CONTENTS

READ A BOOK A WEEK

When you buy a cassette or CD, one of the incidental pleasures is the accompanying booklet. In a few well-chosen words it gives a way into the experience: notes on music and performers, background information, and above all the note-writer's viewpoint, a reaction which you can admire or shout at, as you choose.

Books, by contrast, are usually noteless. Hardback blurbs give away as little as possible, and are sometimes written by people who have never read the actual books. Paperback covers print critical raves, a list of other titles, a bar code and a picture – pretty but useless. No notes; no dialogue.

That's where *Read a Book a Week* comes in. It introduces 52 books, one for each week of the year. As well as description, background, comment, author-biography, sample, there are lists and suggestions for follow-ups. The idea is to give some idea of what to expect if you don't know the book, and something to agree or disagree with, if you do. Five extra sections (Crime and Thrillers; Fantasy and Horror; Science Fiction and Fantasy; Short Stories; Romance of the Past) give hints on particular kinds of reading, with lists, descriptions and samples of their own. Some of the suggested books are classics, others aren't. Each was chosen not for being a highbrow 'must' or a best-selling blockbuster, or both, but because it's one of the best of its particular kind, and should give pleasure; guaranteed.

As the book evolved, it became obvious that anyone who *did* read all the suggested books in a year would have little time left for eating, sleeping or the other joys of life. So *Read a Book a Week* is intended as a menu of reading, not a guide-book or syllabus. There are staple dishes, snacks, specialities and surprises: the idea is to pick and choose. Our advice is to select, dip in and out, feel free. And above all, enjoy.

Thanks to Valerie McLeish, who researched and drafted several entries, and to Kate Newman, who edited the book for press and tracked down permissions.

Kenneth McLeish

Douglas Adams

The Hitch Hiker's Guide to the Galaxy (1979)

● ● ● ● ● ● ● ● ● ● ● ● ● ● ● ● ●

THE STORY

Having escaped from Earth, Arthur Dent and Ford Prefect hitch their way across the universe, protected from its weirdness only by two towels and the infuriatingly know-it-all electronic book *The Hitch Hiker's Guide to the Galaxy*, which (for example) tells everything you need to know about the Ravenous Bugblatter Beast of Traal except how to stop it eating you.

> **ADAMS, Douglas Noel**
> **British citizen**
> **Born 1952**
> **First job: jokewriter**
> **Began writing: 1970s**
> **Other details: as an**
> **impressionable lad, involved**
> **with both *Doctor Who* and**
> ***Monty Python's Flying***
> ***Circus.***

━━━ ━━━ ━━ ━━━ ━━ ━━━ ━━━ ━━

In Adams' universe, infinite improbability rules. Everything is possible; anything can happen. Doors have personalities and mood-swings – and tell us about them. To understand an alien language, you stick a fish in your ear. Mice are the most intelligent creatures in the universe. For entertainment, jaded executives visit the Restaurant at the End of the Universe, watch the floorshow (the End of Everything), then time-travel back to an earlier age and carry on exactly as before.

More seriously, this is a universe where your entire planet can be blasted out of existence to make way for a hyperspace bypass. This is what happens to Arthur Dent one morning, before he has time to dress in anything more stylish than a Marks and Spencer dressing gown. Fortunately, the friend he thought was from Guildford is actually from the planet Betelgeuse, and whisks him away from Earth in the last millisecond before it is vaporized.

Arthur and his friend Ford Prefect become galactic hitch-hikers, using the electronic thumb built into the book *Hitch Hiker's Guide to the Galaxy* for which Ford is a field researcher – and which outsells all competition because it has the words 'Don't Panic' written on it in large letters. The two travellers aren't proud: they take lifts on Vogon battle-cruisers, the Heart of Gold spaceliner hi-jacked by Zaphod Beeblebrox, President of the Universe, and the Ark full of hairdressers and telephone sanitary engineers sent from Earth to find and colonize some planet as yet innocent of clean telephones and advanced coiffure.

Hitch Hiker's Guide to the Galaxy started as a radio series, then became six TV programmes and a 'trilogy' which so far contains five books. It spawned cassettes, videos and an official towel. Each manifestation has its devotees: the radio series is most imaginative; the TV series has best special effects; the books have jokes and incidents not present in the other forms; the towel is fluffiest. An Official Health Warning points out that hitch-hiking is addictive, that if you try just one format you may end up experimenting with all of them. Adams can seriously affect your funny-bone.

OTHER ADAMS BOOKS
Adams has written two books about Dirk Gently, a down-at-heel private detective in a universe subject to the rules of the 'fundamental interconnectedness of all things' – ie one in which coincidence is compulsory. This universe is not the best place to look for logical clues to murder, but he does his best. Time travel, pizzas, and an electric monk whose job is to believe everything, bulk large. The books are *Dirk Gently's Holistic Detective Agency* and *The Long Dark Teatime of the Soul.*

See also
Pratchett, Science Fiction and Fantasy

> 'Night's falling,' he said. 'Look, robot, the stars are coming out.'
>
> From the heart of a dark nebula it is possible to see very few stars, and only very faintly, but they were there to be seen.
>
> The robot obediently looked at them, then looked back. 'I know,' he said. 'Wretched, isn't it?'
>
> 'But that sunset! I've never seen anything like it in my wildest dreams ... the two suns! It was like mountains of fire boiling into space.'
>
> 'I've seen it,' said Marvin. 'It's rubbish.'
>
> 'We only ever had the one sun at home,' persevered Arthur. 'I come from a planet called Earth you know.'
>
> 'I know,' said Marvin. 'You keep going on about it. It sounds awful.'
>
> 'Oh no, it was a beautiful place.'
>
> 'Did it have oceans?'
>
> 'Oh yes,' said Arthur with a sigh, 'great wide rolling blue oceans ...'
>
> 'Can't bear oceans,' said Marvin.

Margaret Atwood
The Handmaid's Tale (1985)

● ● ● ● ● ● ● ● ● ● ● ● ● ● ● ● ●

THE STORY

Offred is a Handmaid: her job is to bear children for state officials whose marriages are barren. She tells us about one 'placement', from the moment she is chosen, to the moment she is removed. During the telling, she spells out for us the details of a society where dogma has replaced memory, where cruelty and secrecy rule, and where human individuality, feeling and emotion are ruthlessly suppressed.

> **Atwood, Margaret**
> **Born 1939**
> **Canadian citizen**
> **Began writing: 1960s**
> **Other details: fascinated by wilderness and its effects on people and animals who live there.**

OTHER ATWOOD BOOKS

Cat's Eye
Surfacing
Life Before Man
Wilderness Tips

TRY THESE

Angela Carter, *The Passion of New Eve*
George Turner, *The Sea and Summer*
Bernice Rubens, *Our Father*
Lynne Reid Banks, *Children at the Gate*

See also

Science Fiction and Fantasy, Tyler

Whatever people in the rest of the world may say, Western historians present the twentieth century as a period of (generally successful) struggle for liberty of every kind. Democracy not dictatorship, social equality, freedom from religious dogma – ours has been a century, we think, of crusades for all such ideals.

Our longing for freedom has also made us fascinated with its opposite. More than any generation before us, we are avidly interested in atrocity, oppression and repression. And because of Freud, we also know how important it is to open up our secret selves. Darkness and nightmare lie, not just in the outside world, but inside our skulls.

Atwood's characters are deeply concerned with the balance, often in the same person, between light and dark, between self-confident freedom and nightmare. Her main characters are usually women. They have all the benefits which Western democracies offer (at least some of) their citizens. But their freedom is also a kind of trap. They can do anything, but find it hard to choose. The openness of their lives terrifies them: it produces a psychological panic like the fear some people feel in vast, empty spaces.

Atwood's books are set in contemporary North America. The surroundings are familiar and comfortable – and this increases each leading character's panic, as she feels that uncertainty and darkness of soul are somehow abnormal, against the grain. *The Handmaid's Tale* reverses this.

In this book, set in the near future, North America has become Gilead, a police state ruled by fanatical religious fundamentalists. All laws derive from the Bible, and the slightest deviation brings punishment without appeal.

In this Hell on Earth, every aspect of 'real' US life is turned on its head. Instead of plenty, there is rationing. Instead of individual freedom, there is state control. Instead of fair trial, there is arbitrary punishment. Above all, women are oppressed. They are denied individuality, and identified only by their usefulness to the state: cook, cleaner, jailer, breeder. They are allowed no books, no free conversation, no choice of clothes, friends, work, emotion, thought; no self.

Novels about totalitarian dictator-ships are common. The oppression of women is an age-old theme. In many cultures, real-life fundamentalist religion is as intolerant as anything Atwood describes. Her inspiration was to put all these themes together, to set her book not in some exotic foreign country but in the 'land of the free' – and to balance this with her leading character's memories of teenage happiness in the 1980s, before the coup: days when college, music and human relationships gave a focus to her life.

Offred, Atwood's 'heroine', is not a striking person: not witty, talented, thoughtful or dynamic. She is perfectly ordinary – and this, in her appalling situation, is Atwood's most chilling idea of all.

● ●

66 From each, says the slogan, according to her ability; to each according to his needs. We recited that, three times, after dessert. It was from the Bible, or so they said. St Paul again, in Acts.

You are a transitional generation, said Aunt Lydia. It is the hardest for you. We know the sacrifices you are being expected to make. It is hard when men revile you. For the ones who come after you, it will be easier. They will accept their duties with willing hearts.

She did not say: Because they will have no memories, of any other way.

She said: Because they won't want things they can't have. 99

JANE AUSTEN
PRIDE AND PREJUDICE (1813)

● ● ● ● ● ● ● ● ● ● ● ● ● ● ● ●

THE STORY

Mr and Mrs Bennet have five grown-up daughters, and Mrs Bennet is delighted when two rich bachelors move into the neighbourhood. She plans marriages. The young people circle each other, politely and with fluctuating degrees of interest. Other characters (boring Mr Collins, snobbish Lady Catherine de Bourgh, snide Miss Bingley, caddish Wickham) divert the course of true affection, and Wickham's behaviour in particular causes trouble between Elizabeth, the Bennets' second daughter, and proud Mr Darcy. It takes an elopement, a trip to the Lakes and an enormous amount of sparky, witty conversation before the story reaches the conclusion every reader has been hoping for since the book began.

> **AUSTEN, Jane**
> **1775-1817**
> **British citizen**
> **Began writing: 1780s (first novel published in 1811)**
> **Other details: wrote *A History of England* ('by a partial, ignorant and prejudiced historian') at 15.**

OTHER AUSTEN BOOKS

Emma
Mansfield Park
Persuasion
Sense and Sensibility
Northanger Abbey

Austen's novels are social comedies. They describe the lives of (fairly) wealthy people at the beginning of the nineteenth century. Her characters are not grand, not the highest of 'high society'. But they have enough money not to need to work, and spend their days devising ever more delightful ways to pass the time.

In this etiquette-bound society, men and women are like beings from two quite different worlds. Men are interested in politics and sport if they are young, books and wine if they are older. Women are interested in relationships, their own and other people's: making them, breaking them and discussing them.

For both sexes, social activity is the hub of existence: visiting friends and relatives, playing cards, gossiping and dancing. In fact all life is like a formal dance, with strict and detailed rules. You can follow the rules or break them, but either way they 'fix' your personality, your reputation and the kind of life you lead.

More than anything else, Austen's characters, male and female alike, work for, concentrate on and respond to marriage plans. A 'good' marriage can transform the lives not only of the partners but of two whole circles of relations; a 'bad' marriage can bring misery and disgrace; to have no marriage at all is (if you are a woman) to have no role in society, and (if you are a man) no peace.

All this may sound restricted and snobbish. But within her chosen boundaries, Austen reveals more depth and range of human character than other writers find in the whole wide world. She unfolds each character gradually: as in real life, we discover someone's personality step by step.

This flower-like revelation of character takes time. At first, the pace of Austen's books seems not so much slow as placid, as if she were showing us a tapestry, stitch by stitch. But every page, every paragraph, has hidden claws. For all her quietness, she has a sharp-eyed view of human foolishness, innocence and pretension – and that, too, is revealed delicately, wittily and precisely as each book proceeds. It may take a few pages to get used to her pace. But after that the novels should seem hypnotic, a never-failing joy.

TRY THESE
Anthony Trollope, *The Warden*
William Thackeray, *Vanity Fair*
Mrs Gaskell, *Wives and Daughters*
Edith Wharton, *The Custom of the Country* (set in 1910s New York)
Angela Thirkell, *The Brandons* (set in 1930s England)

See also
Brontë, Dickens, Du Maurier, Heyer, Romance of the Past, Trollope

Unfinished works and a sequel
Austen left several unfinished novels, and they have been completed by others and published in this century. Examples are *Sanditon* and *The Watsons* (both 'by Jane Austen and Another Lady'): not as good as undiluted Austen, but well worth reading. Joan Aiken's *Mansfield Revisited* (a sequel to *Mansfield Park* by a modern author) is superbly Austenish.

66 'Come here, child,' cried her father, as she appeared. 'I have sent for you on an affair of importance. I understand that Mr Collins has made you an offer of marriage. Is it true?' Elizabeth replied that it was. 'Very well. And this offer of marriage you have refused?'

'I have, sir.'

'Very well. We now come to the point. Your mother insists upon your accepting it – is it not so, Mrs Bennet?'

'Yes, or I will never see her again.'

'An unhappy alternative is before you, Elizabeth. From this day you must be a stranger to one of your parents. Your mother will never see you again if you do not marry Mr Collins, and I will never see you again if you do.' 99

CHARLOTTE BRONTË
JANE EYRE (1847)

● ● ● ● ● ● ● ● ● ● ● ● ● ● ● ●

THE STORY

Jane Eyre, a spirited orphan, is sent by harsh relatives to a remote boarding school, where she ends up as a teacher. She goes as governess to Thornfield Hall, and falls in love with its owner, Mr Rochester. On their wedding day she discovers that he already has a wife: a madwoman living in the attic. She takes refuge with the kindly Rivers family, unexpectedly inherits a fortune, and is sought-after as a bride. Then, driven by sudden impulse, she returns to Thornfield, and finds the Hall burned to the ground, the first wife dead and Rochester humbled and blind. She marries him, and lives fulfilled at last.

BRONTË, Charlotte
1816-1855
British citizen
First jobs: schoolteacher;
governess
Began writing: at the age
of 8; first publication
(poems) 1846
Other details: books
originally published under
the male pen-name
'Currer Bell'.

See also

Austen, Dickens, Du Maurier, Fowles, Romance of the Past

In 1840s England, if you'd asked the average man about women's emotional life, he would have been as surprised as if you'd enquired about trees or chickens. In particular, it would have horrified most men to discover that women had sexual needs or feelings. Women were vessels. Their role was to accept, to satisfy. A man might have the ideal woman in mind, an object to aspire to, but it was a laughable idea that a woman might have in mind the ideal man.

Biographical novels, tracing their characters' lives and thoughts from childhood onwards, were a favourite nineteenth-century form. But the 'heroes' of most such books were men. *Jane Eyre* was one of the first novels to describe a woman's life in this way, and to deal directly with her 'inner landscape': the way she felt, thought and reacted to events.

If male readers of the time were surprised by the notion that women might have an 'inner landscape' at all, they must have been even more taken aback by the sort of things Jane thinks and feels. From childhood (when the book starts) she is a person in her own right, someone of spirit who refuses to accept what she doesn't think right – and if this leads to trouble, ready to take the consequences, to suffer for her own integrity. (Male novels at the time were full of chaps doing this.)

It must be said that Brontë herself had no feminist or liberationist plan when she wrote the book. Her interest was not women's rights, but the personality and development of her principal character.

Jane's picture of herself (the book is told in the first person) is enthralling and believable. What happens to her may be determined by the conditions of women's life in the nineteenth century. But the wishes, hopes, feelings and reactions she describes are so realistic that she seems, so to speak, timeless: we feel that we ourselves might react to similar situations in just these ways.

OTHER BRONTË BOOKS
Shirley (about a Yorkshire mill-owner and the lonely parson's daughter who loves him)
Villette (about an English schoolteacher in Brussels who falls in love with a waspish French professor)

TRY THESE
Emily Brontë, *Wuthering Heights* (in 'older-fashioned' English, sometimes hard to follow, but equally romantic and dream-like)
Jean Rhys, *Wide Sargasso Sea* ('prequel' to *Jane Eyre* by a modern writer, telling the early life of the first Mrs Rochester, and why she went mad)
Daphne Du Maurier, *Rebecca*

● ● ● ● ● ● ● ● ● ● ● ● ● ● ● ● ●

66 The wind roared high in the great trees which embowered the gates; but the road as far as I could see, to the right hand and the left, was all still and solitary: save for the shadows of clouds crossing it at intervals, as the moon looked out ...

A puerile tear dimmed my eye while I looked – a tear of disappointment and impatience: ashamed of it, I wiped it away. I lingered; the moon shut herself wholly within her chamber, and drew close her curtain of dense cloud: the night grew dark; rain came driving fast on the gale.

'I wish he would come! I wish he would come!' I exclaimed. 99

Peter Carey
Oscar and Lucinda (1988)

● ● ● ● ● ● ● ● ● ● ● ● ● ● ● ● ●

THE STORY
In the 1860s, Oscar Hopkins finances his Oxford education by gambling, and is then 'called' by God to go to Australia. Lucinda Leplastrier, meanwhile, uses her inheritance to buy a Sydney glass-works: she hopes (in vain) that her employees will treat her as an equal. Like Oscar, she is a compulsive gambler, and this shared passion brings them together. Their relationship lurches on its awkward, mismanaged way, until the culminating gamble which ends the book.

> CAREY, Peter
> Born 1943
> Australian citizen
> Began writing: 1970s
> Other details: *Oscar and Lucinda* won the 1988 Booker Prize.

OTHER CAREY BOOKS
Illywhacker
Bliss
The Tax Inspector

TRY THESE
Patrick White, *Voss*
Brian Moore, *Black Robe*
Howard Jacobson, *Redback*
Robertson Davies, *What's Bred in the Bone* (self-contained second novel in 'Cornish' trilogy)

See also
Carter, Fowles, Franklin

From the 1820s onwards, Europeans flocked to settle in Australia. Unlike the convicts (whose ships they sometimes shared) they travelled there by choice – and one of the main things which attracted them about Australia was its sense of psychological (as well as geographical) virginity.

If white settlers (who knew nothing of native Australian culture) had been asked to explain this feeling, they might have contrasted their 'new' continent with the 'old' one they had chosen to leave behind. European civilization and culture were elderly. Whatever you chose to do or think, someone had been there before.

In (white) Australia, by contrast, there were no such boundaries. As an immigrant, you might well take European concepts with you, as part of your intellectual luggage – but what you did with them once you landed was up to you. Some new Australians slavishly tried to remake the continent in Europe's image. Others cheerfully junked every aspect of the past.

Carey is fascinated by the openness of possibility offered by a 'new' continent, and by its effect on the people who settle there. His characters are psychologically simple, not sophisticated: adults who approach the experiences of life with the innocence of children. They think everything an adventure – not just work or their social lives, but every emotional experience. When they feel happy, it is to them as if no one else in the world has ever had such a sensation. When they fail in what they try, they may at first be spiritually crushed, but soon spring back and turn eager attention somewhere else.

Some critics compare Carey to no less a novelist than Dickens. This is not because of his style (which is fast and up to date), but because of his plots and characters. He gives people life in a few vivid words of description or a snatch of dialogue. He crams his plots, building a sequence of apparently small incidents (hilarious or sad) into a complex and meaningful pattern.

Above all, Carey rivals Dickens for sheer imaginative scope. He takes a collection of outlandish-seeming ingredients – in this book they include evangelical religion, leeches, flying foxes, gambling, women's rights, and a prefabicated glass church – and gives each a place which seems as inevitable as it is satisfying. As the story proceeds, the main characters, Oscar and Lucinda, move gradually together. To mature as human beings, they must come to terms with the pull they feel between the conventions they were brought up in and the raw opportunities Australia offers them. Their relationship with each other helps this maturing process, but is also a recurring, inescapable stumbling-block. The way they work all this out, in the hothouse combination of restriction and freedom which is mid-nineteenth-century Sydney, is the novel's theme.

● ●

66 Sol brought his craft into the wharf, sliding it gently through the smaller craft, like a careful hand amongst bobbing apples. Lucinda stood up. The crinoline cage swayed ... She gave Mr Myer sixpence for the journey. He gave her a cauliflower and then, in a bristly rush, a kiss on her cold cheek ... Lucinda walked like someone unused to shoes. She struggled up the hill from the wharf with her suitcase banging against her right side, a cauliflower clutched in her left hand ... This is how she arrived at Petty's Hotel. At first they thought her at the wrong address. She placed her cauliflower on the desk and asked them, blushing brightly, if there was a reliable library close to the hotel.

She had decided to study glass. 99

ANGELA CARTER
NIGHTS AT THE CIRCUS (1984)

● ● ● ● ● ● ● ● ● ● ● ● ● ● ●

THE STORY

Walser, freelance US reporter, goes to London to interview the famous bird-woman, Fevvers. Is she freak or fraud? Either way, the story is juicy with scandal and will make his name. As Fevvers tells him of her early life – found in the rushes, brought up in a brothel, wings sprouting at puberty, learning to fly – he is mesmerized by her, and when she sets off on a circus tour of Russia he disguises himself as a clown and follows her. What happens next, especially between Grik, Grok and Chicken Man and between Walser, Samson and Mignon (beautiful, battered waif-wife of Ape-Man), almost distracts our attention from raucous, raunchy Fevvers. Almost – but she has other tricks up her spangled sleeve, other uses in mind for her stunning, (possibly) superhuman powers.

> CARTER, Angela
> 1940-1992
> British citizen
> Began writing: 1960s
> Other details: lived in Japan
> for two years.

OTHER CARTER NOVELS
The Magic Toyshop
Heroes and Villains
The Infernal Desire Machines of
 Doctor Hoffman
Wise Children

Where do stories come from? Why do we respond to them? The psychologist Jung said that the human race has a 'collective unconscious', a memory of our species' whole past experience built into the structure of the brain. Other writers say that stories, especially myths and folk-tales, tap into this experience – which is why they have such power. We also reach into this unconscious in dreams, whose images are more profound and meaningful to us than the filtered reality of the everyday.

Carter wrote non-fiction about this, and one of her most spectacular fiction books (*The Bloody Chamber*) was a collection of folk-tales (eg 'Red Riding Hood') retold in a dreamlike, sensual and unsettling way. She was also interested in how sexual feelings underlie our psychological make-up and program our behaviour, and how such feelings affect the different ways women and men experience, and control, their lives.

All this is a rich mixture, exploring 'difficult' emotional and intellectual territory. Fortunately, by the time it got into Carter's novels, all difficulty had long been left behind. She had a rich, rollicking imagination, stuffed like a cupboard, and grabbed story-ingredients from it like a cook on speed – a snippet of folk-tale, a spoonful of sex, a pinch of politics – until the final concoction is unique, aromatic and irresistible.

Nights at the Circus is brash, rude, gaudy and irrepressible. Fevvers, the heroine, is a nineteenth-century trapeze artist who may or may not be half bird, a woman hatched from an egg. She is mysterious, coarse, shrewd, prim, lewd and vulnerable. She carries a dagger like a sting: a secret weapon against the legion of dirty old men whose one aim, in her words, is to 'pop her cherry'. Her story is a farcical odyssey from the brothels and freak-shows of Victorian London to a circus tour of Tsarist Russia, a mad, wild land where primitive superstition rubs noses with up-to-the-minute political treachery, where ghosts, shamans and intelligent apes mix on equal terms with humans, and where Dark Forces (tigers, lust, armed revolution) are forever plucking at Life's curtains and threatening to burst centre-stage.

TRY THESE
Bamber Gascoigne, *The Heyday*
David Cook, *Sunrising*
Alejo Carpentier, *Baroque Concerto*
Jeanette Winterson, *The Passion*
Jenny Diski, *Rainforest*

See also
Carey, Dickens, Fowles, Morris

66 'I took refuge in a nearby spinney, in the top branches of an elm, where I startled a sleepy congregation of rooks. When I got my breath back, I peered out to see what was afoot below and saw Mr Rosencreutz's bullies, now dressed as gamekeepers, beating the undergrowth for me, so I stayed put till night came on again. Then I went from covert to covert, always concealing myself, until I came to the railway line and borrowed a ride off a load of freight, climbed in amongst a truck of taters and pulled a tarpaulin over my head, because, at that time, I was not able to fly so high the clouds might hide me, and I can think of few things more conspicuous, even by night, than a naked woman dodging telegraph wires and hopping over signal boxes – for I needed the railway to guide me back to London.' 99

CRIME AND THRILLERS

The first fictional sleuth, Augustin Dupin, was created by Edgar Allan Poe 150 years ago, and Sherlock Holmes, perhaps the most famous of all invented detectives, followed 50 years later. Since then crime novels have featured 'great detectives' of every kind, as well as moving out to cover private eyes, routine police work and the 'capers' of criminals themselves. Thrillers began with the adventure novels of writers like Walter Scott and R.L. Stevenson. Many are war stories, or deal with the activities of spies and counterspies. (This last kind took a battering when the Cold War ended in 1989, and US–USSR espionage became a no-go fictional area. The spy novel is currently groggy but recovering.) Many crime and thriller writers also produce scripts for TV detective and adventure series, so that we know their work even before we read their books.

RUTH RENDELL (born 1930) writes under her own name and as 'Barbara Vine'. Her own books are of two types: placid police procedurals starring Chief Inspector Wexford (*An Unkindness of Ravens*), and tense, Highsmithish stories of paranoia and obsession (*The Tree of Hands*). Her 'Barbara Vine' books (*A Fatal Inversion*) are denser novels, in which crime is only part of a complex web of relationships.

DONALD E. WESTLAKE (born 1933) writes hilarious 'caper' novels: descriptions of meticulously planned crimes which go spectacularly wrong. Recommended titles: *The Hot Rock*; *Bank Shot*; *Jimmy the Kid*; *Help! I Am Being Kept Prisoner*.

TED ALLBEURY (born 1917) wrote some of the best Cold War spy thrillers. Recommended titles: *The Man With the President's Mind*; *The Crossing*; *The Secret Whispers*.

DICK FRANCIS (born 1920) writes thrillers about blackmail, fraud and murder among jockeys, owners, trainers and others in the racing business. Recommended titles: *Blood Sport*; *Bonecrack*; *Slay-Ride*; *Whip Hand*.

'ED McBAIN' (Evan Hunter, born 1926) writes tough police procedurals set in the 87th Precinct of the New York Police Department. Recommended titles: *Cop Hater*; *Let's Hear it for the Deaf Man*; *Shotgun*; *Fuzz*.

ROBERT B. PARKER (born 1932) has completed Chandler's unfinished novel *Poodle Springs*, and has written a score of novels about a Chandlerish private eye of his own, Spenser. Recommended titles: *Playmates*; *Looking for Rachel Wallace*; *Ceremony*.

FREDERICK FORSYTH (born 1938) writes dazzling adventure thrillers. Recommended titles: *The Day of the Jackal*; *The Dogs of War*.

See also

Dexter, Doyle, Greene, Highsmith, Hope, le Carré, Leonard, Paretsky, Simenon, Stevenson

TRY THESE
THRILLERS
Daniel Easterman, *The Ninth Buddha*; Len Deighton, *Berlin Game*; Ian Fleming, *Doctor No*; Jack Higgins, *The Eagle Has Landed*; Geoffrey Household, *Rogue Male*; Jonathan Kellerman, *Over the Edge*; Robert Ludlum, *The Icarus Agenda*; Wilbur Smith, *Shout at the Devil*

CRIME

Robert Barnard, *Bodies*; Peter Dickinson, *The Seals*; Sue Grafton, *A is for Alibi*; Reginald Hill, *An Advancement of Learning*; John Milne, *Shadow Play*; Ross Macdonald, *The Drowning Pool*; Joseph Wambaugh, *The Glitter Dome*

VINTAGE CRIME

Margery Allingham, *More Work for the Undertaker*; Raymond Chandler, *Farewell My Lovely*; Agatha Christie, *Murder at the Vicarage*; Carter Dickson, *The Red Widow Murders*; Hilda Lawrence, *Death of a Doll*; Ngaio Marsh, *A Surfeit of Lampreys/Death of a Peer*; Margaret Millar, *Wall of Eyes*; Rex Stout, *Too Many Cooks*

" From *Prizzi's Glory* by Richard Condon (born 1915):
On Tuesday morning he called Charley at the laundry in Brooklyn. Charley gave the high sign to Al Melvini to put a trace on the call, then he let 220 seconds go by before he picked up.
'Yeah?' Charley said. 'Too bad about Vanni and Saul.' 'Whatta you want me to tell you?'... 'Listen, we can settle everything. I musta been crazy. I got hot and now I regret it. I wanna put in a bid for the franchise.'
'You got till tomorrow like everybody else. Send in your bid.'
'I wanna have a meet.'
(Other Condon books: Prizzi's Honour; Prizzi's Family; The Manchurian Candidate; The Vertical Smile) "

" From *A Taste for Death* by P.D. James (born 1920):
'My son was murdered. The police will know that soon if they don't already. And I know it now.'
He said: 'Forgive me, but can you be sure? All Barbara could tell me when she rang this morning was that the police had found Paul's body and that of a tramp,' he paused, 'with injuries to their throats.'
'Their throats were cut. Both their throats. And from the careful tact with which the news was broken, I imagine that the weapon was one of Paul's razors. I suppose Paul could have been capable of killing himself. Most of us are, given sufficient pain. But what he wasn't capable of was killing that tramp. My son was murdered, and that means that there are certain facts the police will make it their business to discover.'
He asked, calmly:
'What facts, Lady Ursula?'
'That you and Barbara are lovers.'...
(Other James books: An Unsuitable Job for a Woman; The Skull Beneath the Skin; Devices and Desires) "

COLIN DEXTER
THE DEAD OF JERICHO (1981)

●●●●●●●●●●●●●●●●●

THE STORY

Morse meets a pretty girl twice: at a party, and as a corpse. The rich mixture of the story also contains two hyper-bright sixth-formers, a peeping Tom, adultery, business corruption and blackmail. The setting is Jericho, a warren of shabby Victorian streets bounded by the Radcliffe Infirmary, Worcester College, the cemetery and the sour canal.

DEXTER, Colin
Born 1930
British citizen
First jobs: schoolteacher (classics), Senior Assistant Secretary to Oxford Delegacy of Local Examinations (supervising what used to be called 'O' and 'A' Levels)
Began writing: 1975
Other details: regular competitor, and frequent champion, in national crossword-puzzle competitions.

OTHER DEXTER BOOKS

His name is simply Morse. (He has a rarely-used initial, E., but no known name to go with it.) He is a Detective Chief Inspector in the Oxford CID, and is the latest in a line of 'classic' detectives, beginning with Sherlock Holmes and including such luminaries as Hercule Poirot, Peter Wimsey and Nero Wolfe.

Morse solves murders partly by legwork – clambering over walls, peering at corpses, interrogating suspects – and partly by incandescent brain-power. He can focus his mind away from everyday matters to concentrate on the evidence, as he might home in on a crossword puzzle or a chessgame. During this process he likes to play grand opera, loud, on his hi-fi system – and woe betide anyone who interrupts.

Morse is a middle-aged bachelor, with a fondness for real ale, fine art, vintage cars and soft pornography. He is rumpled, short-tempered and (in the books, though less so on TV) moody. His most trusted friend is his colleague, the down-to-earth family man Lewis, though Morse would sooner die than let Lewis realize this.

Lewis plays Doctor Watson to Morse's Holmes: Morse confides in him, thus keeping us slower-witted readers abreast of his thinking. Lewis' ordinariness and niceness also keep Morse (and us) in touch with everyday people, and lead to flashes of inspiration too simple for Morse's lofty brain. (In several books, it is Lewis who works out the essential detail which sets Morse's mind racing to solve the case.)

There is a third main 'character' in every

book: Oxford. Most Oxford writers concentrate on the colleges. But Dexter is little interested in undergraduates, punting and vintage port. His Oxford is the city itself: its dark old streets and churches, its boarding houses, factories, pubs and shopping malls. Morse loves Oxford, the place; if the University and everyone connected with it were transported to Mars, he would shed few tears.

With such characters and such a setting, Dexter can hardly fail as a 'classic' detective writer. The clinching factor is the way he plans his plots. They are puzzles, to be experienced step by step. We see each clue as Morse does; we are given hints and nudges about the way he is thinking; we are all but invited to run ahead of him and solve the crime. We never do, of course, because there is always at least one twist within a twist. Reading a Morse story is like playing a game of skill with the man himself.

TRY THESE
P.D. James, *A Taste for Death*
Sheila Radley, *Who Saw Him Die?*
Reginald Hill, *An Advancement of Learning*
Robert Barnard, *Bodies*

'CLASSIC' DETECTIVES
Michael Innes, *Operation Pax/Paper Thunderbolt*
Ngaio Marsh, *A Surfeit of Lampreys/Death of a Peer*
Margery Allingham, *Flowers for the Judge*
Edmund Crispin, *The Moving Toyshop*

See also
Crime and Thrillers, Doyle, Simenon

66 The weapon was settled then, and Morse felt he ought to put his colleague on the right lines about motive, too.

'Whoever killed him was pretty obviously looking for something, don't you think, Bell? And not just the address of some deaf-and-dumb nymphomaniac, or the results of the latest pike-angling competition.'

'You think he found what he was looking for?'

'I dunno,' said Morse.

'Well, I'll tell you one thing. We've been over the house with a nit-comb, and – nothing! Nothing that's going to help us. Fishing tackle galore, tools, drills, saws – you name it, he's got it in the do-it-yourself line. So what, though? He goes fishing most days, and he does a few handyman jobs round the streets. Good luck to him!'

'Did you find a trowel?' asked Morse quietly. 99

CHARLES DICKENS

NICHOLAS NICKLEBY (1839)

● ● ● ● ● ● ● ● ● ● ● ● ● ● ● ● ●

THE STORY

Nicholas, his sister Kate and his mother, left penniless when the father dies, throw themselves on the mercy of Ralph Nickleby, a harsh financier. He sends Nicholas to work at Dotheboys Hall, a Yorkshire boarding school run by the aptly-named Wackford Squeers. Horrified by the way Squeers brutalizes the children, Nicholas rescues Squeers' chief victim (Smike) and runs away. They join a band of touring actors. In the meantime, Ralph Nickleby has set Nicholas' sister Kate to work in a dress-shop, and arranges for one of his uncouth friends to make advances to her. It is up to Nicholas to get back to London, sort all this out and find a way to support his family – and in the process, he falls in love.

DICKENS, Charles John Huffham
1812-1870
British citizen
First jobs: factory worker (aged12); office-boy; reporter
Began writing: 1830s
Other details: spent much time touring Britain and US, reading from his works.

MORE DICKENS BOOKS
Oliver Twist
David Copperfield
Great Expectations
The Pickwick Papers

Most of Dickens' books were first published as serials, in weekly magazines. There were between twenty and forty episodes and it was not until the last was published that the whole thing was gathered together in book form. Thus, the author had two bites at the financial cherry – and his work also catered for two kinds of readers: those who liked the stories short with gaps between, and those who preferred their fiction in chunkier form.

Nowadays we belong to the second group. We prefer to buy novels as single, complete books. Serial fiction is uncommon, though it does exist. But there is a modern form of serial-telling, organized in weekly or part-weekly episodes: TV and radio soaps.

Dickens assembled his novels in much the same way as modern TV soap-writers create their scripts. He began by choosing half a dozen strong situations and characters (or groups of characters). A poor, honest widow who is incurably chatty, and her likeable son and daughter. A crooked financier and his business cronies. A boarding school run by a slimy sadist. A touring actors' company. An easy-going business run by two kindly, merry brothers. (All these examples come from *Nicholas Nickleby*.)

Once these main ingredients were devised, Dickens could begin. He chose one or two of them for each episode, breaking off story-strands in the middle, coming back to them, rounding them off or sending them in unexpected new directions – again, exactly as modern soap writers work.

Dickens started his writing career as a journalist. He produced newspaper accounts of trials – and specialized in brisk word-pictures of the people involved: defendant, judge, watchers in the gallery, court officials. These 'snapshots in words' are also a feature of his novels. Each character is so vividly described that some are now better known than the books they come from.

Dickens' novels are long, and take their time. They contain not only description, but slapstick, melodrama and savage attacks on the social and political corruption of Victorian England. Each can be read at one gulp or approached in the way he favoured himself: in instalments, a chapter or section at a time. That approach, especially for people new to him, gives his work time to settle in, to haunt the mind.

TRY THESE
William Thackeray, *Vanity Fair*
Mrs Gaskell, *Mary Barton*
H.G. Wells, *Kipps*
David Cook, *Sunrising*

STEALING UP ON DICKENS
Dickens' busy plots and dazzling characters make him a favourite author for adaptations. Stage versions range from the RSC's 1980 *Nicholas Nickleby* to such hit musicals as *Oliver!* and *Pickwick*. Films run the gamut from *Great Expectations*, directed by David Lean, to the Disney version of *A Christmas Carol*. All the novels have been adapted as TV serials, and most are available on video.

See also
Austen, Brontë, Carey, Carter, Fowles, Trollope

● ● ● ● ● ● ● ● ● ● ● ● ● ● ● ●

66 'Do you reject these terms, sir?' inquired Mr Gregsbury, with his hand on the bell-rope.

'I fear so, sir,' replied Nicholas.

'That is as much as to say that you had rather not accept the place, and that you consider fifteen shillings a week too little,' said Mr Gregsbury, ringing. 'Do you decline it, sir?'

'I have no alternative but to do so,' replied Nicholas.

'Door, Matthews!' said Mr Gregsbury, as the boy appeared.

'I am sorry I have troubled you unnecessarily, sir,' said Nicholas.

'I am sorry you have,' rejoined Mr Gregsbury, turning his back on him. 'Door, Matthews!'

'Good morning, sir,' said Nicholas.

'Door, Matthews!' cried Mr Gregsbury. The boy beckoned Nicholas, and tumbling lazily downstairs before him, opened the door, and ushered him into the street. With a sad and pensive air he retraced his steps homewards. 99

Arthur Conan Doyle

The Hound of the Baskervilles (1902)

●●●●●●●●●●●●●●●●●

THE STORY

The inhabitants of a remote, lonely moor tell the legend of a huge black beast with fiery eyes. It howls in the mists, and its howls mean death. After the 'hound' is blamed for the mysterious death of Sir Henry Baskerville, Holmes is called in (with Watson in attendance) to track down the beast and solve the crime (if there is a crime) before the monster can strike again.

> Doyle, Arthur Conan
> 1859-1930
> British citizen
> First job: doctor
> Began writing: 1880s
> Other details: worked as doctor on an Arctic whaling ship; fascinated by spiritualism and the paranormal.

THE 'REAL' SHERLOCK HOLMES

Doyle based Holmes on two real people. His genius for scientific detection was inspired by Doyle's old tutor in medicine, Dr Joseph Bell of Edinburgh University, a master of diagnosis. Holmes' flamboyant manner was inspired by the actor Sir Herbert Tree, a wit of Doyle's own day. (Tree once saw a man struggling to carry a grandfather clock along the street, stopped him and said, 'If I were you, my dear fellow, I'd use a watch.')

One of the most amazing things about Sherlock Holmes is that many people think him real. Sackfuls of letters arrive at 'his' address (actually a building society's): 221b Baker Street, London. Correspondents not only beg him to solve crimes, but ask advice on problems of family, money, sex, world politics. Few other fictional characters get fan mail: who but a maniac would expect answers from Elizabeth Bennet, Bertie Wooster or Gandalf the White?

In Doyle's stories, Holmes is a 'consulting detective', a kind of upper-class private eye. He lives in lodgings run by Mrs Hudson and shared by his friend Dr Watson (who narrates the stories). He takes on cases where the police are baffled or useless, and is often at loggerheads with the dogged but unimaginative Inspector Lestrade.

When Doyle invented Holmes, scientific detection was a new idea. Instead of relying on hunches or 'information received', Holmes examines the evidence in minute detail. From hairs on a jacket, the amount of wear on a shoe-heel, the colour of someone's cheeks, the length of a fingernail, he can deduce a whole lifestyle, an entire history. The more baffling the case, the more Holmes' skills come into play – the idea of detection as a kind of intellectual gymnastics is crucial to the book's success.

Doyle's greatest invention, however, was Holmes' own character. Holmes is a master performer, at ease everywhere, from gangland pub to Buckingham Palace. He plays the violin, speaks a dozen languages, reads philosophy for pleasure – and suffers from deep, romantic melancholy, a 'wound which cannot be healed' and which he never reveals. He is a connoisseur of wine, food, tobacco and – Doyle's contemporaries were surprisingly unshocked by this – cocaine. He struts through life like a pop star on a stage. Watching the way he works is as pleasurable as trying to second-guess the mental feats by which he solves each crime.

By the street-smart standards of some modern detective stories, Doyle's English is a little old-fashioned. But as soon as Holmes sets to work, you forget this. He is so seductive, such a dazzler, that he makes all later detectives seem like shadows.

DOYLE'S HOLMES BOOKS
A Study in Scarlet (novel)
The Sign of the Four (novel)
The Valley of Fear (two-part story)
Adventures of Sherlock Holmes, Memoirs of Sherlock Holmes, The Return of Sherlock Holmes, His Last Bow, The Casebook of Sherlock Holmes (short-story collections)

TRY THESE
Nicholas Meyer, *The Seven-per-cent Solution* (about Holmes)
Richard L. Boyer, *The Giant Rat of Sumatra* (about Holmes)
G.K. Chesterton, *The Innocence of Father Brown*
John Dickson Carr, *The Emperor's Snuff Box*

See also
Crime and Thrillers, Dexter, Simenon

66 I was at Holmes' elbow, and I glanced for an instant at his face. It was pale and exultant, his eyes shining brightly in the moonlight. But suddenly they started forward in a rigid, fixed stare, and his lips parted in amazement. At the same instant Lestrade gave a yell of terror and threw himself face downwards on the ground. I sprang to my feet, my inert hand grasping my pistol, my mind paralysed by the dreadful shape which had sprung out upon us from the shadows of the fog. A hound it was, an enormous coal-black hound, but not such a hound as mortal eyes have ever seen. Fire burst from its open mouth, its eyes glowed with a smouldering glare, its muzzle and hackles and dewlap were outlined in flickering flame. Never in the delirious dream of a disordered brain could anything more savage, more appalling, more hellish, be conceived than that dark form and savage face which broke upon us out of the wall of fog. 99

DAPHNE DU MAURIER

REBECCA (1938)

● ● ● ● ● ● ● ● ● ● ● ● ● ● ● ●

THE STORY

The story-teller, while acting as companion in Monte Carlo to a snobbish rich woman, meets handsome Maxim de Winter. They fall in love, marry, and he takes her back to Manderley, his house in Cornwall. The young, shy bride at first puts the hostility she finds everywhere down to her own inadequacy. All is hints and suggestions; nothing is ever said openly – except by Mrs Danvers, the sinister housekeeper, who tells the girl to her face that she is no match for Rebecca, Maxim's first wife, now dead. Then, just when the tension seems to have been screwed as tight as it will go, a body is found ...

- DU MAURIER, Daphne
- 1907-1989
- British citizen
- Began writing as a young teenager
- Other details: family came to Britain during French Revolution; her grandfather was an author, her father a famous actor; she wrote a 'family biography', *The Du Mauriers*, as fascinating as any of her fiction.

OTHER DU MAURIER ROMANCES
Jamaica Inn
Frenchman's Creek
My Cousin Rachel
Mary Anne

Rebecca's first sentence, 'Last night I dreamt I went to Manderley again', is one of the most famous openings in literature. It sets the mood of unreality and apprehension which permeates the story. Throughout the novel we see everything through the unnamed heroine's eyes. She never feels truly in control of events; she is more like a spectator, like someone blundering in a dream – and Du Maurier subtly, without a wasted word, makes us feel that we share each trembling step, experience each thudding heartbeat. When the heroine is told that her husband is a murderer, it is like a hammer-blow to us as well as to her.

'Gothic' stories, in nineteenth-century romance, involved young women exploring dark, lonely old houses, and coming to suspect their handsome, mysterious new husbands of terrible crimes – until the nerve-wracking quest was over and the truth was known. In the twentieth century, this kind of physical quest was replaced by the 'psychological novel', whose characters explore not houses but their own uncertainties and fears.

Like most Du Maurier novels, *Rebecca* blends these two ideas. The more the heroine explores Manderley, the sinister house to which her new husband brings her, the more she discovers about his past, his character and herself. Throughout, she has a strong feeling that she is in physical as well as psychological danger – and each time she makes a discovery which dispels her fear, something else happens and brings it looming back. The last third of the book, when she is sure that her husband is a killer, is a kind of detective story – except that the clues the girl finds unravel not just crime, but her own confused and panic-stricken state.

It is a feature of dreams that even when you know how they end, you can dream them again, with exactly the same sense of helplessness and dread as you felt the first time through. This happens to *Rebecca*'s heroine. The end of the book is not the end of the story: it doubles back on itself, starts again (as the first line suggests) as if nothing has happened to change it. For readers, this is also one of the most haunting things about the novel. When you turn from the last chapter back to the first, to check how the dream began, you do not find everything clearer than it was before, but even more mysterious.

TRY THESE
Philippa Gregory, *The Favoured Child*
Susan Howatch, *Penmarric*
Frank Yerby, *A Woman Called Fancy*
Catherine Darby, *Rowan Garth*

See also
Carey, Fowles, Romance of the Past, Tyler

66 'The bishop's wife wants to know when we are going to give a Fancy Dress ball at Manderley?' I said, watching him out of the tail of my eye. 'She came to the last one, she said, and enjoyed it very much. I did not know that you have Fancy Dress dances here, Frank.'

.... He looked a little troubled. 'Oh yes,' he said after a moment, 'the Manderley ball was generally an annual affair. Everyone in the county came. A lot of people from London too. Quite a big show.'

'It must have taken a lot of organisation,' I said.

'Yes,' he said.

'I suppose,' I said carelessly, 'Rebecca did most of it?' I looked straight ahead of me along the drive, but I could see his face was turned towards me, as though he wanted to read my expression.

'We all of us worked pretty hard,' he said quietly. There was a funny reserve in his manner as he said this ... 99

DOROTHY DUNNETT
NICCOLÒ RISING (1986)

● ● ● ● ● ● ● ● ● ● ● ● ● ● ● ● ●

THE STORY

The background to *Niccolò Rising* is banking, trading and intrigue as sixteenth-century Europe becomes one of the world's great trading continents. Home base is a dye-works in Bruges, the hub of northern European trade. Marian de Charetty, a widow, heads the Charetty Company, which as well as trading has begun to hire out its own private army, and becomes increasingly involved in international politics and espionage. The story unfolds through the eyes of a number of young men, one of them Marian's own son – and gradually begins to focus on the mesmeric, charismatic figure of Niccolò himself.

> **DUNNETT, Dorothy**
> **Born 1923**
> **British citizen**
> **First job: civil servant**
> **Began writing: 1961**
> **Other details: a well-known portrait-painter.**

The 'House of Niccolò' series
Niccolò Rising
The Spring of the Ram
Race of Scorpions
Scales of Gold
(two more in the pipeline)

The sixteenth century was one of the most turbulent, kaleidoscopic periods in European history. All over the continent, medieval ways and ideas were giving way to the dazzling light of the Renaissance. Science, religion and the arts were spinning off in heady new directions. Explorers were opening people's eyes to the facts that the world was round, and that it had continents and countries which beggared imagination. It was a sprawling, excitable time, a carnival of enlightenment and barbaric cruelty, colour and corruption, spectacle and squalor.

Dunnett's historical novels revel in every political, religious, social, mercantile and artistic detail of this century of seething change. She plunges with relish into the whirlpool of European (and Levantine, and Asian) affairs. There are two six-book series. The 'Lymond' books fan out from Scottish border squabbles to take in England, France, Malta and beyond. The 'House of Niccolò' series moves from Belgium to the towers of Trebizond.

With such vast areas to cover, Dunnett wastes no time on scene-setting. At the beginning of each series, she showers you with a score of locations, a hundred plot strands, a cast of thousands. The first fifty pages or so can seem bewildering, but she has everything in hand. It is as if you are being shown a vast, crammed tapestry on a wall: at first a blur, but growing ever clearer and more fascinating as you take in more detail.

Dunnett's way of showing us character

is equally distinctive. Many novelists spend pages on description, slowing down the narrative while we take in each character's appearance and personality. Dunnett, by contrast, likes to show us each person, each event, through the eyes of other people in the story. We never pause long enough to absorb more than fleeting detail. But after a while, things we glimpse in one place remind us of what we have read pages, even chapters, before. We build up our own impression from a mass of small details as the book proceeds.

This method works especially well for Dunnett's heroes. At first they are enigmatic and elusive. But getting to know them is like exploring someone's personality in real life: each new piece of information fills another chink in our knowledge, until our picture is gorgeously, gloriously complete.

THE 'LYMOND' SERIES
The Game of Kings
Queen's Play
The Disorderly Knights
Pawn in Frankincense
The Ringed Castle
Checkmate

TRY THESE
Tom de Haan, *A Mirror for Princes*
Jean Plaidy, 'The Plantagenet Saga' (beginning with *The Plantagenet Prelude*)
Thomas B. Costain, *The Silver Chalice*
Rafael Sabatini, *The Sea Hawk*

See also
Carey, Graves, Renault, Romance of the Past, Winterson

66 The cold eyes remained on her face. 'You sound, madame,' said the Vicomte de Riberac, 'as if you were no friend to our noble young Scotsman.'

She stared him back. 'Then you are right,' said Katelina. 'I happen to think him – to know him – to be a self-indulgent, vindictive rake.'

'So I thought. What a pity it all is,' said the fat French nobleman, and heaved a deep sigh ... Somewhere, trumpets sounded. The conversation in the great hall began to lessen. People moved, to make way for the controller, for the Dauphin, for the brother of the King of Scots. People began to take their places to walk, two by two, to the banquet. Only around one small group did complete silence fall; did no one move ...

'What a pity,' repeated the fat man, with no emphasis. 'For – perhaps I should have told you? Forgive me if I did not think to tell you – your self-indulgent, vindictive rake ... really? How very sad! – is my son.' 99

GERALD DURRELL
MY FAMILY AND OTHER ANIMALS (1956)

●●●●●●●●●●●●●●●●

THE STORY

Mother settles with her family on Corfu. They live in a succession of villas as Larry's circle of friends and Gerry's animal collection keep growing. Larry, a would-be avant-garde writer, fills the house with arty friends, who talk philosophy, make eyes at Margo and shudder every time they come into contact with raw Nature (usually something crawly or slithery from Gerry's collection). Gerry sails his boat, walks with Roger his dog – and never stops believing (such is the innocence of childhood) that his family will one day share his enthusiasm for millipedes, magpies, lizards, wasps, mice, snakes ...

DURRELL, Gerald Malcolm
Born 1925
British citizen
First job: assistant zookeeper
Day job: naturalist
Began writing: early 1950s
Other details: pioneered the idea, now world-wide, of breeding rare animals in captivity and reintroducing them to the wild when numbers are viable.

Durrell was brought up on the island of Corfu in the 1930s, long before the days of mass tourism. Corfu was then a serene place, the home of peasant farmers and shepherds and of a few outsiders – not least of them the Durrell family: indulgent Mother, Larry the twenty-year-old genius, Leslie with his passion for boats and guns, Margo with her passion for young men, and wide-eyed, accident-prone Gerry (aged about nine).

There being no suitable schools on Corfu, Gerry had a succession of private tutors, who did their best to teach him the basics of history, geography and the three Rs. But he spent most of his time exploring the island, talking to people, 'collecting' their memories and characters, and studying every kind of animal from butterfly to blenny, from gecko to little owl. He describes Corfu as a kind of paradise: the weather is always summer, human beings are eccentric and hilarious, and the animals are mysterious, characterful and endlessly fascinating.

This is a trick either of memory or of writing skill. Durrell is one of those people we think must have led truly exciting lives, so much less predictable than our own. In fact all he does is look at the ordinary from an extraordinary point of view. If we consider the people and animals in our own lives – shopkeepers, relatives, pets, birds in the trees – and then imagine them viewed through Durrell's eyes, they immediately become unique. It is simply a matter of adjusting the way we see the world. His book is no tedious progression of facts, like a general's or politician's memoirs. Imagination transforms it; its glow comes from him alone.

My Family and Other Animals is special for three things above all. First is the sequence of slapstick set-pieces, involving Gerry's touchy brothers and sister, or his tutors' bizarre ideas of how to educate a growing boy. Second is his loving account of the way animals look and behave: leaf-carrying ants; a scorpion nursing its young; a toad gulping moths; the courtship of tortoises. Third is the way he colours his memories with adult irony, adult nostalgia, an adult perception of how bizarre human beings can be. Durrell makes us nostalgic for his nostalgia, makes his reality seem the only one possible. It is a rare quality, and it transforms his book.

66 The family, assembled on the verandah, viewed Mother's prize as it waddled up the path towards them, eyes bulging, minute legs working frantically to keep the long, drooping body in motion, ears flapping wildly, pausing now and then to vomit into a flower-bed.

'Oh, isn't it sweet?' cried Margo.

'Good God! It looks like a sea-slug,' said Leslie.

'Mother! Really!' said Larry, contemplating Dodo with loathing. 'Where did you dig up that canine Frankenstein?'

'Oh, but he's sweet,' repeated Margo. 'What's wrong with him?'

'It's not a him, it's a her,' said Mother, regarding her acquisition proudly. 'She's called Dodo.'

'Well, that's two things wrong with it for a start,' said Larry ... 'Just look at it! Look at the shape! How did it get like that? Did it have an accident, or was it born like that?' 99

FANTASY AND HORROR

Fantasy and horror have always been popular. Myths and folk tales swarm with ghouls, giants, wizards and other magic creatures, and their plots are usually quests or contests between light and dark. 'Psychological' horror fiction began in the 1840s with the work of Edgar Allan Poe. Instead of facing supernatural monsters, his characters fight the madness and terror inside their own heads. Modern horror writers such as James Herbert and Stephen King often combine the two types, supernatural and psychological, in the same stories. Fantasy writing was boosted in 1955 by Tolkien's *The Lord of the Rings*, and is now a major style of fiction. It ranges from simple sword-and-sorcery epics (whose nickname explains their contents) to more complex stories involving 'inner' as well as 'outer' quests. Many writers blur the edges between fantasy and horror, to satisfying effect.

MERVYN PEAKE (1911-1968) wrote the Gothic-horror 'Gormenghast' trilogy, *Titus Groan*, *Gormenghast* and *Titus Alone*.

CLIVE BARKER (born 1952) began as a writer of straightforward blood-chillers (collections: six *Books of Blood*). In 1987, with *Weaveworld*, he began a series of novels combining horror with fantasy, set in the miniature, deadly kingdom of the title.

STEPHEN DONALDSON (born 1947) is best-known for his 'Thomas Covenant' series, adventure-fantasy inspired by – and better than – *The Lord of the Rings*. There are six books in two absorbing trilogies, the first beginning with *Lord Foul's Bane* and the second with *The Wounded Land*.

EDGAR ALLAN POE (1809-1849) was the great-great-grandfather of the horror story, and is still among the most gruesome of all horror authors. His stories are collected in *Tales of Mystery and Imagination*.

STEPHEN KING (born 1946) is the modern master of supernatural horror, known especially because of the blockbusting films made from many of his novels. Titles include *Carrie*, *Salem's Lot*, *The Shining*, *Pet Semetary*, *It*, *Misery* and *The Dark Half*.

ANNE MCCAFFREY (born 1926) wrote poetic, mystic fantasies set in the magic land of Pern, which is controlled by gentle, music-loving and telepathic dragons. Recommended titles: *Dragonflight*, *Dragonquest*, *Dragonsong*.

BRAM STOKER (1847-1912) invented Count Dracula, the man who turns to a vampire bat at night and drinks human blood. Endlessly mocked and parodied, his original book (in diary and letter form) can still be one of the most frightening novels ever written.

See also
Pratchett, Tolkien

TRY THESE

FANTASIES

Piers Anthony, *A Spell for Chameleon*

Peter Beagle, *The Last Unicorn*

Raymond Elias Feist, *Magician*

Barbara Hambly, *The Time of the Dark*

Fritz Leibner, *The Swords of Lankhmar*

R.A. Macavoy, *Damiano*

Patricia A. McKillip, *The Riddle-Master of Hed*

Tim Powers, *The Anubis Gate*

CHILLERS

Virginia Andrews, *Flowers in the Attic*

Robin Cook, *Mutation*

Stephen Gallagher, *Oktober*

James Herbert, *Moon*

H.P. Lovecraft, *At the Mountains of Madness*

Dean R. Koontz, *Whispers*

Mary Shelley, *Frankenstein*

Bram Stoker, *Dracula*

66 From *Pawn of Prophecy* by David Eddings (born 1931):

'There's the boy!' a voice rang out from behind them, and Garion whirled. Two men were running down the street toward him, one with a sword and the other with a wicked-looking curved knife. Knowing it was hopeless, Garion raised his club, but Silk was there. The small man launched himself from the shadows directly at the feet of the two, and all three crashed to the street in a tangle of arms and legs. Silk rolled to his feet like a cat, spun and kicked one of the floundering men solidly just below the ear. The man sank twitching to the cobblestones. The other scrambled away and half-rose just in time to receive both of Silk's heels in his face as the rat-faced Drasnian leaped into the air, twisted and struck with both legs. Then Silk turned almost casually.

'Are you all right?' he asked Garion.

'I'm fine,' Garion said. 'You're awfully good at this kind of thing.'

'I'm an acrobat,' Silk said. 'It's simple once you know how.'

(*Pawn of Prophecy* is the first book in the Belgariad sequence. Eddings' best-known other fantasy-sequence is the Malloreon books) 99

GUSTAVE FLAUBERT
MADAME BOVARY (1857)

●●●●●●●●●●●●●●●●●

THE STORY

Emma Bovary's marriage, to a dull provincial doctor, is routine and boring, nothing like the romantic dreams she had as a young girl. She tries to ignite her life by conducting love-affairs under her husband's nose – and finds that they, too, quickly pall. She runs up huge debts, buying presents for her lovers, and furniture and decoration for her gloomy house. When her creditor sends in bailiffs, the house of cards which is Emma's view of herself comes crashing round her ears.

> FLAUBERT, Gustave
> 1821-1880
> French citizen
> Other jobs: none (private income)
> Began writing: early teens
> Other details: had a 'mistress' whom he contacted only by letter; was a doctor's son, and a hypochondriac.

TRY THESE

Honoré de Balzac, *Eugénie Grandet*
Stendhal, *Scarlet and Black*
Nikolai Tolstoy, *Anna Karenina*
Anthony Trollope, *The Small House at Allington*

▬ ▬ ▬ ▬ ▬ ▬ ▬ ▬

See also
Dickens, Fowles, Trollope, Twain

Flaubert was an extraordinarily obsessive man. He spent every day at his desk, working neurotically and surrounded by objects – pen-holders, paperweights, cushions, a stuffed parrot – which were essential to his psychological and creative state.

He claimed to hate the status of 'famous writer' which his writing brought him – but it never crossed his mind to give the profession up for something else.

Flaubert's second obsession was social. He despised his own class, the provincial middle class, to the point where he stayed indoors, refusing to meet people and hearing about their doings (with loathing, one presumes) at second hand from his relatives and servants. Knocking the bourgeoisie was a favourite pastime of French intellectuals in the 1850s, but Flaubert took it to extremes. He disliked some of his characters so much that he wrote extra scenes (not for publication) subjecting them to as many ludicrous, shameful or painful ordeals as he could devise.

Finally, Flaubert was a perfectionist about his style – far more than most writers. He set out to give an exact impression or description of everything he wrote, to 'become' (as he said in a letter) not only each character but also 'the leaves, the wind, the horses'. He wanted to eliminate commentary, to let his chapters flow as neutrally, as objectively, as a river. Producing prose which did its job without drawing any attention to itself took hours of effort. It could take two weeks to produce a single page.

In *Madame Bovary,* all Flaubert's obsessions come together to produce a masterpiece. Its subject is the self-destructive stupidity of the middle class. Its method, piling up incident after incident, plunges us into the lives of Emma Bovary, her husband, her lovers, her servants, as directly as if we knew them personally. We are filled with alarm and pity for the characters; we are as involved as if the events were happening in our own back yard and before our eyes.

OTHER FLAUBERT NOVELS
Sentimental Education (about a man's hopeless love for a married woman)
Salammbô (historical novel set in ancient Carthage)
The Temptation of St Anthony (experimental novel, modelled on a painting by Brueghel, and attempting to give a word-panorama of all the temptations which can beset a devout believer)

66 Rodolphe leant back against the marquee. He was thinking so hard about Emma that he heard nothing. Behind him, servants stacked dirty dishes on the grass. His neighbours spoke to him; he didn't answer. Despite the hubbub all round him, his mind was filled with a great silence. He dreamt of what she'd said, the shape of her lips, her face glinting in the soldiers' cap-badges as if in a magic mirror. The tent walls reminded him of the folds of her dress; ahead of him, long days of love stretched to infinity down the vistas of the future.

That evening, he saw her again, at the firework display. But she was with her husband, Madame Homais and the chemist (who was in a panic about the danger of unexploded bangers, and kept rushing off to give Binet the benefit of his advice).

Thanks to over-caution, the fireworks delivered to Monsieur Tuvache had been stored in the cellar. The powder was damp and slow to light, and the main attraction, a dragon biting its tail, was a total failure. Now and then, desultory rockets flared – and each time the gaping crowd sent up a cheer, mingled with the squeals of women who were being goosed in the darkness. Without speaking, Emma snuggled gently against Charles' shoulder, lifting her chin as she followed the rocket-trails in the dark sky. Rodolphe gazed at her in the lanterns' glow. 99

MARGARET FORSTER
LADY'S MAID (1990)

● ● ● ● ● ● ● ● ● ● ● ● ● ● ● ●

THE STORY
Wilson, a young woman from
Newcastle, goes to London to
become lady's maid to the invalid
genius Elizabeth Barrett. At first the
two women are wary, but gradually
Barrett is captured by Wilson's
warmth and sincerity, and Wilson is
warmed by Barrett's combination of
mental steel and physical
helplessness. Each 'grows' as a
human being because of the
relationship. Then Robert Browning
meets Barrett, and the lives and
relationship of Wilson and Barrett
are forever changed.

> ○ FORSTER, Margaret
> ○ **Born 1938**
> ○ **British citizen**
> ○ **Began writing: 1960s**
> ○ **Other details: has written**
> ○ **biographies of Elizabeth**
> ○ **Barrett Browning, of eight**
> ○ **pioneering women**
> ○ (*Significant Sisters*)
> ○ **– and of a man who thought**
> ○ **he was God's gift to the**
> ○ **female sex, Bonnie Prince**
> ○ **Charlie.**

See also
Carey, Dickens, Fowles, Romance
of the Past

───────────────────

OTHER FORSTER NOVELS
Private Papers
Marital Rites
Mother Can You Hear Me?
Georgy Girl

The Barretts of Wimpole Street was one of
the biggest stage and film successes of the
1930s. It told of Elizabeth Barrett, the second daughter in a large middle-class
Victorian family, of her tyrannical father
and of the dashing young poet who wooed
and carried her off in the teeth of all oppo-
sition.

It was a grand piece of work, with juicy
parts for everyone. (Charles Laughton, as
Mr Barrett, was at his eye-rolling best.)
Unfortunately, there was hardly a word of
truth in it. Recent research has shown that
Elizabeth Barrett was nothing like the
melodramatic heroine the film depicts, and
that her father's efforts to protect her came
more from fear for her life (she was chroni-
cally sick) than from bloody-minded bully-
ing. Her marriage to Browning was one of
the literary events of the age.

In *The Barretts of Wimpole Street*, a
minor part is played by Barrett's faithful
maid, Wilson. *Lady's Maid* now tells
Wilson's story – the true facts – as a historical novel. And it is as surprising and as
moving as anything invented for stage or
film.

In *Lady's Maid*, the real 'affair' is not
between Barrett and Browning, but
between Barrett and Wilson. The relationship is intellectual and emotional, but
never sexual. We watch Wilson grow in
stature, from the uneducated country girl of
the start to the mature, confident person she
becomes as the story proceeds. We see the
Barrett–Browning relationship from
Wilson's point of view, and the book mov-

ingly shows how it affects Wilson's own relationship with Barrett, and her perception of her own importance in the world.

In this book, Forster manages the rare trick of showing someone growing and changing over some forty years. She also provides fascinating detail of the 'upstairs-downstairs' life of a large Victorian household. She writes smoothly, patiently, like someone building a wall with words instead of bricks. The novel is warm, human and unfussy. It is about how even the most ordinary-seeming people are unique, and its persuasive quietness makes all the huffing and puffing of the stage-show and film seem a flashy waste of time.

SERVANTS
There are few novels about servants. But many true-life accounts, often by people who used to be in service, give pictures of life 'below stairs'. Margaret Powell's *Below Stairs* describes a household similar to the Barretts' when Wilson worked there. Monica Dickens' *One Pair of Hands* is funny about her days as 'cook-general' to a succession of wildly different employers. Céleste Albaret's *Monsieur Proust* is the story of the woman who kept house for Marcel Proust.

They stopped outside Mr Kenyon's lovely house and Timothy came out directly. 'Why, it is Timothy, is it not?' Miss Elizabeth cried. 'Do you remember Timothy, Wilson?'

'Of course, miss, now do take care with your gown or it will catch in the door again.' Bending down, Wilson fussed over the dress, neatly covering her own embarrassment. But Timothy was being wicked.

'And I remember Mrs Wilson, Miss Barrett,' he said as he carried their basket up the steps, 'for how could I forget when she kept us all in order?'

'Good gracious, Timothy,' Miss Elizabeth said lightly, 'I have never seen Wilson as a tartar.'

'Oh, I did not mean that, miss, she is too pretty to be a tartar.'

It was outrageous and Wilson was furious. Timothy was laughing and smiling but Miss Elizabeth was not. She went quiet and held her head a little higher; if Timothy only had the wit to see this was a sign that she thought he was being impertinent, as indeed he was.

JOHN FOWLES
THE FRENCH LIEUTENANT'S WOMAN (1969)

● ● ● ● ● ● ● ● ● ● ● ● ● ● ● ●

THE STORY

Charles Smithson, a rich young man, goes to to pass the summer of 1867 in Lyme Regis, on the English south coast. He intends to dig for fossils there, and to spend time with his fiancée, Ernestina Freeman. Early in his stay, however, he meets the mysterious 'French Lieutenant's Woman', Sarah Woodruff, and as the summer passes he becomes obsessed – first by the secret of her life, and then by her personality. This leads him to discover things about his relationship with his fiancée, about stuffy Victorian middle-class society, and about himself; the result is violent, irrevocable change.

FOWLES, John
Born 1926
British citizen
First job: schoolteacher
(French)
Began writing: 1950s

TRY THESE

Gustave Flaubert, *Madame Bovary*
William Thackeray, *Vanity Fair*
Lawrence Durrell, *The Dark Labyrinth/Cefalù*
D.M. Thomas, *The White Hotel*
Robertson Davies, 'The Cornish Trilogy'

This novel was filmed in 1979, starring Meryl Streep and Jeremy Irons, with a screenplay by Harold Pinter. Pinter recast the book as a film within a film. We saw two things happening at once: the story set in the nineteenth-century which was being filmed, and the twentieth-century director, cast and crew who were making that film.

This 'double vision' almost exactly matches what Fowles does in his novel. The book's heart is a straightforward nineteenth-century story, told in a nineteenth-century way. Its characters' ways of speaking, thinking and behaving never once stray out of period.

Fowles himself, however, is not so constrained. As he tells the story, he keeps breaking out of it to tell us things. He comments on what his characters have just said or done, reflects on their motives, compares their attitudes with those of later generations. He discusses political, literary and social ideas of which they can have had no possible knowledge. Above all, he keeps on talking of the book he is writing, the book we are reading – of what may happen next, of possibilities he has rejected, of how, with a stroke of the pen, he can wipe out what we have just read.

Fowles' presence in his own book gives it a cheerful, chatty tone: it is easy and smooth to read. The story comes to seem almost like a living thing, changing and growing as we read. And Fowles' comments fix the nineteenth-century characters in their period, framing them, as it were, by showing us their place in history.

This 'framing' is vital, since the story depends on mid-Victorian attitudes to society and sex. Nowadays we think completely differently about both – and Fowles uses modern attitudes to shed helpful light on his invented people and events. The book's heroine, for example, the 'French Lieutenant's Woman' of the title, exists both as a character in her own right, and – Fowles reminds us – as a symbol of the sexual licence and moral freedom which his hero longs for and finally achieves at the expense of ...

But is it 'at the expense of' anything – and if so, of what? Like all conjurors, Fowles keeps his cleverest trick till last. He supplies two entirely different endings. Neither is the one we have been led to expect, and neither is final.

OTHER FOWLES BOOKS
A Maggot
The Magus (revised version)
Daniel Martin
The Collector

GRAND PASSIONS
Leo Tolstoy, *Anna Karenina*
Colette, *The Ripening Seed*
Margaret Mitchell, *Gone With the Wind*

See also
Brontë, Carey, Dickens, Forster, Trollope

66 And now let us jump twenty months. It is a brisk early February day in the year 1869. Gladstone has in the interval at last reached No 10 Downing Street; the last public execution in England has taken place; Mill's Subjection of Women and Girton College are about to appear. The Thames is its usual infamous mud-grey. But the sky above is decisively blue; and looking up, one might be in Florence.

Looking down, along the new embankment in Chelsea, there are traces of snow on the ground. Yet there is also, if only in the sunlight, the first faint ghost of spring. I am ver ... I am sure the young woman whom I should have liked to show pushing a perambulator (but can't, since they did not come into use for another decade) had never heard of Catullus, nor would have thought much to all that going on about unhappy love even if she had. But she knew the sentiment about spring. After all, she had just left the result of an earlier spring at home (a mile away to the west) and so blanketed and swaddled and swathed that it might just as well have been a bulb beneath the ground ... 99

MILES FRANKLIN
MY BRILLIANT CAREER (1901)

● ● ● ● ● ● ● ● ● ● ● ● ● ● ●

THE STORY

Sybylla, daughter of a shrew and a drunkard, longs to escape from farm and family life. She spends a few blissful months with her wealthy grandmother in Sydney, but then is recalled to earn money for the family, and goes to teach the children of a boorish outback family to whom her father owes money. Her life is further complicated because she has a suitor who offers the escape of marriage, but who will only accept her as a subservient wife, not an equal partner. Sybylla tells us every thought, every feeling as she fights her way through the tangle of her life towards the brilliant career she longs for.

○ FRANKLIN, Miles
○ 1879-1954
○ Australian citizen
○ Real name: Stella Maria
○ Sarah Miles Franklin
○ First jobs: domestic servant;
○ journalist
○ Began writing: 1890s
○ Other details: other pen
○ names were 'Mary Anne' and
○ 'Brent of Bin Bin'.

OTHER FRANKLIN BOOKS

My Career Goes Bung (sequel)
Childhood at Brindabella
    (autobiography)
All that Swagger
Old Blastus of Bandicoot

Franklin's own story is as amazing as her novel. She grew up on a smallholding in New South Wales, the eldest of a family of seven. She wrote *My Brilliant Career* at sixteen, and was highly embarrassed when, after it was published five years later, her family and neighbours assumed it was autobiography, and took offence. She forbade republication until after her death, and when the book reappeared in the 1950s it was hailed as 'the first Australian novel' and a work of female emancipation years ahead of its time.

Franklin was a pioneer radical and feminist. She left Australia in 1906, worked for ten years for the US Women's Trade Union League, nursed in Greece in the First World War, and spent fourteen years in London as political secretary for the National Housing Council. She returned to Australia in 1933, and spent the rest of her life working for women's equality and socialist causes, and writing a score of books, including eleven more novels.

Franklin always claimed that *My Brilliant Career* was pure fiction, nothing to do with her own life. Maybe so. But it is written in the first person, by an ardent sixteen-year-old trapped by family poverty (and the fact that she is female) into being a household drudge. The events of Sybylla's life, and her all-or-nothing approach to them (she swings in a moment from ecstatic rapture to the depths of self-loathing and despair), seem uncannily to mirror Franklin's own experience and character.

In 1979, thanks to a film starring Judy

Davis and Sam Neill, *My Brilliant Career* became world-famous. It gives a fascinating glimpse of what is to most readers a remote and exotic world, that of subsistence outback farmers a century ago: hard-working, good hearted – but also bigoted, hide-bound and vulgar. As Sybylla's personality develops – in those days you could be a 'little girl' at sixteen and a 'responsible' wife and mother just a few months later – she sees that to be herself she must tear herself away from her past. This discovery is standard in 'growing-up' novels; but Franklin renders it superbly poignant by making Sybylla as infuriating, charming and natural as if she were sitting beside you as you read.

TRY THESE

Henry Handel Richardson, *The Getting of Wisdom*

Edna O'Brien, *The Country Girls*

Elizabeth Bowen, *The Death of the Heart*

Angela Carter, *The Magic Toyshop*

See also
Carey, Forster, Grass

66 Not believe in God! I was mad!

If there really was a God, would they kindly tell me how to find Him?

Pray! Pray!

I prayed, often and ardently, but ever came that heart-stilling whisper that there was nothing to pray to.

Ah, the bitter, hopeless heart-hunger of godlessness none but an atheist can understand! Nothing to live for in life – no hope beyond the grave. It plunged me into fits of profound melancholy.

Had my father occupied one of the fat positions of the land, no doubt as his daughter my life would have been so full of pleasant occupation and pleasure that I would not have developed the spirit which torments me now. Or had I a friend – one who knew, who had suffered and understood, one in whom I could lose myself, one on whom I could lean – I might have grown a nicer character, but in all the wide world there was not a soul ... 99

JANE GARDAM
THE QUEEN OF THE TAMBOURINE (1991)

● ● ● ● ● ● ● ● ● ● ● ● ● ● ● ● ●

THE STORY

Eliza Peabody lives in a rich South London suburb. She is beautiful, secure in her religion, happily married, and at ease with her neighbours, most of whom she has known for years. Then Joan (a comparative newcomer who lives in the house opposite) leaves her husband. Eliza becomes progressively more and more involved with Joan and her family – and cannot understand why, as events proceed, her concern is not shared by her husband or her neighbours. The book is in the form of letters, from Eliza herself, and this allows Gardam to show every twist and turn from Eliza's own point of view, something vital to the story.

GARDAM, Jane Mary
Born 1928
British citizen
First job: journalist
Began writing: 1970s
Other details: worked for a time in the 1950s as travelling librarian for Red Cross Hospital service.

OTHER GARDAM NOVELS
Bilgewater
God on the Rocks
Crusoe's Daughter

Gardam writes clear, flowing English in short sentences. Her prose seems almost clinical, as if all emotion had been bleached out of it. This is important to the effect of her work, because her books describe the turbulence which comes to people's personalities under pressure. Each of her central characters lives in a secure emotional world – or at least a world whose emotional boundaries are well known and accepted – until something happens and that world is never the same again.

Gardam's cool prose helps in another way. Even as she tells us what is happening, what people are saying, she plants seeds of information on other things, catching their essence in a few clear paragraphs. In *The Queen of the Tambourine*, for example, there is a short scene between the heroine and an old man in a restaurant. A woman, a complete stranger, comes up to them and starts talking about the British attitude to anti-semitism. In what the woman says, and in Gardam's description of her clothes and her manner, we learn more about a certain kind of British snobbery, about anti-semitism – and, in passing, about the main character and her companion – than some other writers would tell us in an entire chapter.

Gardam is good at showing inadequacy and obsession, particularly in the areas of love, sex, religion and madness. In some novels her central characters are young girls, and she superbly describes the roller-coaster of adolescent longing and emotion. Other novels use the main, child character as a window on to the tragic farce of adult behaviour – the child's perception of which changes as the character grows up.

Gardam's plots are often wildly funny, treating life as some kind of surrealist circus. Many writers share this viewpoint, but few also have Gardam's gift of stylistic stillness. The combination of the two makes her books seem gentle and effortless as you read them, but simultaneously unsettling and satisfying afterwards.

TRY THESE
Susan Hill, *The Springtime of the Year*
Anita Brookner, *Look at Me*
Elizabeth Bowen, *The Death of the Heart*
Olivia Manning, *School for Love*
Simon Rees, *Nathaniel and Mrs Palmer*

See also
Godden, Jansson, Jolley, Tyler

"Outside was a bus-stop and a bus coming ... I climbed upstairs so that I could ride between the branches of the sycamores along the Common's edge. There was only one other passenger, sitting on the front seat, too, across the gangway from me. He was a boy, about ten years old ... He had silky hair and the back of his neck under his red and white striped school cap had a heart-breakingly beautiful cleft in it. I wanted all at once to kiss it, then thought that perhaps nowadays that would be called child-abuse. He might report me. Well, so he should. We hadn't been introduced. He'd sock me one.

The boy was reading steadily, page after page of a comic, and as he read, his feet in red and grey woollen socks kicked and swung, kicked and swung. When children stop swinging their legs they're grown up. He stopped and looked at me, then went on reading ... The pages of the comic were lovingly turned and turned. When he gathered up all his things to get off the bus, he looked at me again and gravely raised his cap to me.

Oh, all the different kinds of love –"

RUMER GODDEN

COROMANDEL SEA CHANGE (1991)

● ● ● ● ● ● ● ● ● ● ● ● ● ● ● ●

THE STORY

Anglo-Indian Aunt Sanni runs a hotel on the Coromandel coast. Her devoted staff care for a huge variety of guests, of all nationalities, including a party of American archaeologists, and (central to the story) a young English couple, Blaise and Mary Browne. They have married in haste, are on honeymoon, and are already aware that their relationship is not working. In the world outside the hotel, a feverish election campaign is taking place, and parallels between one of the candidates, Krishnan, and the god Krishna propel the Brownes inexorably from incompatibility to tragedy.

> GODDEN, Rumer
> Born 1907
> British citizen
> First job: teacher (in India)
> Began writing: 1930s
> Other details: also known for
> children's books, books
> of travel and autobiography
> (especially about her time in
> India).

OTHER GODDEN NOVELS
The River
Kingfishers Catch Fire
The Greengage Summer
The Battle of the Villa Fiorita
In This House of Brede

This book is set in modern times, in a hotel on the Coromandel coast of India. Ancient travellers spoke of Coromandel as if it were somewhere not of this world, but a magic place no one could visit without being changed. Coromandel may have been in Shakespeare's mind when he wrote *The Tempest*, set on Prospero's magic island, and *The Tempest* gives this book's title its second half: Ariel in the play sings of a drowned man undergoing 'a sea change, into something rich and strange' – exactly what happens to the characters in Godden's story.

Godden is always at her best writing about people in large groups and close-knit communities. She shows how people respond to the disciplines of their setting, how their lives interpenetrate, as they affect others and are themselves affected. Most of her books have large 'casts', a variety of characters who come and go as the story demands.

Another strand in most Godden novels is the way each central community reacts to the world outside. That world is itself often 'enclosed': a society with its own strict rules and restrictions. This 'background-in-the-foreground' is vital to each book, because what happens in the 'outside' world directly affects the people in the community at the heart of the story. There is usually a huge outside event – in *Coromandel Sea Change* it is an election campaign – which reverberates in the situation and attitudes of every character.

Because Godden is so interested in peo-

ple changing and reacting, she writes especially well about young people and the
clash between different cultures. Many of
her books centre on adolescents or young
adults, crossing the threshold of grown-up
experience. The culture-clash can be
between two different ethical or philo-
sophical systems (for example religious
and secular views of life), or the values of
two different continents (Europe and India
are favourites) or, in her finest books of all,
both at once.

Godden treats all such serious ideas in
an unobtrusive but effective way. Her style
is light, and seems to float on the surface
of life rather than diving deep. But her
underlying themes give substance. You
read her fast, for pleasure – but you may
find her scenes and images impossible to
forget.

GOOD ON INDIA
**Ruth Prawer Jhabvala, *Heat and
Dust***
M.M. Kaye, *The Far Pavilions*
E.M. Forster, *A Passage to India*
**Olivia Manning, *'The Balkan
Trilogy'* (about a young
couple under stress in the
run-up to the Second World
War)**

TRY THESE
Lynne Reid Banks, *Children at the
Gate* (set in Israel)
Elizabeth Bowen, *The Death of the
Heart*

See also
Gardam, Jolley, Tyler

66 The light fell, too, on chests carried on poles laid each side of them and painted scarlet. 'Marriage chests,' said Olga Manning.

She had come out in the late afternoon to watch them play. 'Uninvited,' Blaise had muttered. As soon as they came off the court she had come up to them whereupon he had picked up the racquets and presses and left.

Olga had taken no notice. 'It's for a wedding,' she explained to Mary. 'There must be one near, in some village. This is the bride's dowry being brought down to the bride-groom's house. She must be a hill girl. Poor little thing, proba-bly married to a man she doesn't know,' and Mary, startled, thought, I'm married to a man I don't know. Almost she said it aloud but, as if she had, Olga said with curious passion, 'None of us should marry, unless we love a man so much we would go through hell for him, which we shall probably have to do.' 99

WILLIAM GOLDING
LORD OF THE FLIES (1954)

● ● ● ● ● ● ● ● ● ● ● ● ● ● ● ● ●

THE STORY

A group of boys – six- to thirteen-year-olds, all from the same boarding school – is marooned on a deserted island after a plane crash. There are (at least as far as we and the boys know) no surviving adults. At first the children organize their lives according to hierarchical systems remembered from school, but gradually they degenerate into gangs, fascism and the tyranny of strong over weak. (These, together with the presence of the Devil in the world, are the main themes in all Golding's work.) The end is inevitable: a hunt to the death, and the collapse not merely of 'British' values but of every quality which gives the human race any claims at all to be 'civilized'.

GOLDING, William Gerald
Born 1911
British citizen
First jobs: actor; naval officer; schoolteacher
Began writing: 1930s
Other details: won Booker Prize in 1980 and Nobel Prize for Literature in 1983; wrote comic novel a year later (*The Paper Men*) about a world-famous author on the run from journalists, critics and biographers.

What would British children do if they were trapped, without adults, on a deserted island? One answer is given in one of the best-known children's books of the nineteenth century, R.M. Ballantyne's *Coral Island*. In this, three boys are marooned, and vigorously set about reminding themselves, and us, that they are products of the British public school system. The oldest, Ralph, organizes the others like a prefect bossing fags; schedules and rotas are drawn up, blubbing is outlawed, stiff upper lips are demanded at all times and one constantly wins the battle against panic and homesickness in order to do one's best for God and for the Queen.

Coral Island ran through dozens of editions and affected the thinking of millions of children. Golding, a schoolmaster in the 1950s, judged it both ridiculous and pernicious. He thought that it ignored any idea of the place of evil in human nature, and was therefore particularly irrelevant in a century which had produced two world wars, the Holocaust and the atomic bomb. As he said, 'Anyone who moved through those years without understanding that man produces evil as a bee produces honey, must have been blind or wrong in the head.'

Lord of the Flies shows what Golding thinks real British children might do if marooned. 'Lord of the Flies' is the Bible's name for the Devil, and in Golding's novel, the Devil takes control. Fear, superstition, cruelty and violence scrape off the children's 'civilized' veneer, and they revert to savagery. (In Golding's terms, they rediscover original sin, the fault for which Adam and Eve were expelled from Paradise; in their own way, they re-enact the Fall.)

Unaccountably, *Lord of the Flies* has been set for school examinations almost every year since it was published. Apart from readability, it seems to offer adolescents little: its view of good and evil, the human race, desert islands, is too individual to be used for 'lessons'. But read by adults, its proper audience, it can be devastating. It is grand and uncompromising, in a way we associate less with modern English novelists than with such giants of the past as Zola, Melville or Dostoevsky. But calling Golding a giant is hardly an insult – and giants, in the right circumstances, can be far more stimulating company than pigmies.

TRY THESE
Marianne Wiggins, *John Dollar*
Patrick White, *A Fringe of Leaves*
Susan Hill, *I'm the King of the Castle* John Barth, *Giles Goat-Boy*

OTHER GOLDING NOVELS
The Inheritors
Pincher Martin
The Spire
The Pyramid
Rites of Passage, Close Quarters, Fire Down Below (trilogy)

See also
Carey, Grass, Greene, Irving, Naipaul, Stevenson

● ● ● ● ● ● ● ● ● ● ● ● ● ● ● ● ●

❝ 'There.'

In front of them, only three or four yards away, was a rock-like hump where no rock should be. Ralph could hear a tiny chattering noise coming from somewhere – perhaps from his own mouth. He bound himself together with his will, fused his fear and loathing into a hatred, and stood up. He took two leaden steps forward.

Behind them the sliver of moon had drawn clear of the horizon. Before them, something like a great ape was sitting asleep with its head between its knees. Then the wind roared in the forest, there was confusion in the darkness and the creature lifed its head, holding towards them the ruin of a face.

Ralph found himself taking giant strides among the ashes, heard other creatures crying out and leaping and dared the impossible on the dark slope; presently the mountain was deserted, save for the three abandoned sticks and the thing that bowed.

❞

GÜNTER GRASS
CAT AND MOUSE (1961)

● ● ● ● ● ● ● ● ● ● ● ● ● ● ● ●

THE STORY

Joachim Mahlke is physically all but freakish: he has a huge Adam's apple (the 'Mouse' of the title) and an enormous penis, out of scale with his body. He is almost as much at home in water as on land: an expert swimmer and diver, skilled at exploring (and making dens in) wrecked warships. The novel recounts events from his last three years at school, as he and his friends move from childhood to maturity, from innocence to awareness – and from the fantasy-games of boyhood to the more deadly cat-and-mouse encounters of a country ruled by a dictator and a world at war.

GRASS, Günter
Born 1927
German citizen
First job: graphic artist
Began writing: 1950s
Other details: expert cook.

OTHER GRASS NOVELS

The 'Danzig' trilogy:
The Tin Drum, Dog Years, Local Anaesthetic
Headbirths, or The Germans are Dying Out
The Flounder

See also
Gardam, Irving, Jolley, Tyler

After the Second World War, it was as if the German nation went through an identity crisis. Many people felt as if the Hitler years, culminating in the war, had wiped out their past. The cultural experience of the German-speaking peoples, built up over centuries of history and culture, seemed to have become meaningless.

While industrialists and workers set about economic recovery in the 1950s and 1960s, writers and artists began exploring this phenomenon of identity. What did it mean to be German? Was there a cultural pattern of Germanness – and if so, how did modern, post-war people fit into it? If one considered the Hitler years as a dismal, disastrous aberration, was it possible to recover some cultural self-confidence, some dignity?

Many writers answered these questions in books with strong political or social themes – books which now seem hopelessly dated. Grass took a different line. He played an active part in real politics, but when it came to fiction he drew themes from life and literature at large, from the whole range of German-language culture. In the 1960s he also worked in drama, writing and designing for the 'Theatre of the Absurd'. In this, surrealism rules. The natural world is replaced by dream-reality: anything can happen, and the only demand is that everyone treats every event, however bizarre, as if it is the most humdrum thing imaginable.

Grass uses this kind of absurdism in his novels. He stuffs his books with jokes, set-pieces, songs, recipes, music-hall sketches, political argument, family rows, mock trials – nothing, it seems, is out of place. Readers who like literary roller-coaster rides need look no further.

The hero of *Cat and Mouse* is forever trapped between one state of existence and another. He is an adolescent: neither innocent nor mature. He is at home in water almost as much as on land. He is bisexual. And – this is where Grass slides in the seriousness – he is growing up in 1940s Nazi Germany: too young to fight in the war, but old enough to have clear ideas of what is going on and what he thinks about it. By describing a dozen episodes in his hero's life, at school and on holiday, Grass shows us a whole generation forced to make decisions about its personal and national identity.

TRY THESE
John Irving, *A Prayer for Owen Meany*
Mario Vargas Llosa, *The Time of the Hero/The City and the Dogs*
André Gide, *The Counterfeiters*
J.G. Ballard, *The Unlimited Dream Company*

BETWEEN TWO WORLDS (NOVELS ABOUT GROWING UP)
S.E. Hinton, *Rumble Fish*
J.D. Salinger, *The Catcher in the Rye*
Carson McCullers, *The Member of the Wedding*
Jane Gardam, *Bilgewater*
John Updike, *The Centaur*
Mordecai Richler, *The Education of Duddy Kravitz*
John Irving, *The Hotel New Hampshire*

● ● ● ● ● ● ● ● ● ● ● ● ● ● ●

> ❝ He came shooting upward: bluish-red around the chin, yellowish over the cheekbones. His hair parted exactly in the middle, he rose like a fountain from the hatch, staggered over the bow through water up to his knees, reached for the jutting gun-mounts, and fell watery-goggle-eyed to his knees; we had to pull him up on the bridge. But before the water had stopped flowing from his nose and the corner of his mouth, he showed us his find, a steel screwdriver in one piece. Made in England. Stamped on the metal: Sheffield. No scars, no rust, still coated with grease. The water formed into beads and rolled off. Every day for over a year Mahlke wore this heavy, to all intents and purposes unbreakable, screwdriver on a shoelace. ❞

ROBERT GRAVES
I, CLAUDIUS (1934)

● ● ● ● ● ● ● ● ● ● ● ● ● ● ●

THE STORY

After a long civil war, Rome is settling down as an Empire ruled by a single family. Public politics may be stable, but in private the members of the family bicker, plot and poison each other in the quest for personal power. Claudius is a stammerer and a cripple, and his bloodthirsty relatives think him too feeble-minded to be a threat; he is left alive. He stands on the sidelines of history, watching – and surviving – the murderous antics of his grandmother Livia, his grandfather Augustus, his uncle Tiberius and his cousin the lunatic emperor Caligula. Watching, and waiting ...

GRAVES, Robert von Ranke
1895-1985
British citizen
Began writing: 1916 (while serving in the trenches during the First World War)
Other details: lived much of his life in self-imposed exile from Britain, on Majorca; wrote a complete version of the Greek myths, and controversial books treating Jesus' life as if it were myth.

See also
Dunnett, Renault, Romance of the Past

For centuries, writers, performers and their audiences have been fascinated by ancient Rome. From Shakespeare to the scriptwriter of *A Funny Thing Happened on the Way to the Forum*, from opera composers to Khachaturian (who wrote a ballet about Spartacus), creative artists have taken what they needed from ancient Rome, and had a wonderful time with it.

All these artworks have given the ordinary spectator a very clear notion, true or false, of what ancient Rome was like. Nero fiddling while Rome burned; Christians wrestling lions; aristocrats enjoying orgies or making interminable speeches in the Senate; legions on the march to conquer Asterix and Obelix – such images are known world-wide. But there is another, subtler side to the past, and this is what fascinated Graves.

Earlier creators, even Shakespeare, had treated the Romans as if they were contemporary people who just happened to wear togas and carry swords. The manners were authentic but the thought was anachronistic. Graves, by contrast, was interested in getting as close as possible to 'real' Roman feelings, ideals, likes, dislikes, sense of humour – in short, humanity. He assumed that they might talk about eating, drinking, growing tired, sweating, smelling – even, in one famous passage, farting – just like us. He thought that they might react to their religion, paganism, just as modern believers do to theirs. He imagined that personal relationships were as vital to Romans as they are to us today. He depicted their politics not just as showcase public debates, but as devious affairs of backstage whispering, treachery and intrigue.

The result of all this was not a dry academic text but a fictional bombshell. *I, Claudius* sold in millions, and still does. It makes the plotting, feuding, love affairs and hatreds of Julius Caesar's descendants, the first imperial dynasty of Rome, as immediate as today's tabloid headlines. Claudius (who narrates the story) is no marble statue come lumpishly to life, but a convincing human creation, and the supporting cast is crammed with tyrants, maniacs, fiends, perverts and sycophants. Stir in Graves' own witty, point-scoring style, and how could *I, Claudius* go wrong?

OTHER GRAVES NOVELS
Claudius the God (sequel)
The Golden Fleece/Hercules My Shipmate (about Jason and the Argonauts)
Sergeant Lamb of the Ninth (about the American War of Independence)
Wife to Mr Milton (set during England's civil war)

TRY THESE
Peter Green, *Sword of Pleasure* (ancient Rome)
John Arden, *Silence Among the Weapons* (ancient Rome)
Thornton Wilder, *The Ides of March* (ancient Rome)
Mary Renault, *The King Must Die* (ancient Greece)
Mika Waltari, *Sinuhe the Egyptian* (ancient Egypt)

> Now Tiberius had made a pet of the most extraordinary animal ever seen at Rome. Giraffes excited great admiration when first seen, and so did the rhinoceros, but this, though not so large, was far more fabulous. It came from an island beyond India called Java, and was like a scaly lizard nine feet long with an ugly head and a long darting tongue ... It was called the Wingless Dragon and Tiberius fed it himself every day with cockroaches and dead mice and such-like vermin. It had a disgusting smell, dirty habits and a vicious temper. The dragon and Tiberius understood one another perfectly.

GRAHAM GREENE
BRIGHTON ROCK (1938)

●●●●●●●●●●●●●●●●

THE STORY

Pinkie, also known as The Boy, is a seventeen-year-old gangster in 1930s Brighton. He inherits the gang leadership when the previous leader is murdered by rivals. He tracks down Fred Hale, a journalist he thinks betrayed the former leader, and Hale dies. Pinkie realizes that he has left evidence in a seedy café, and plots to marry the frightened, innocent young waitress, Rose, to prevent her giving evidence in court against him. Meanwhile Ida Arnold, who is in Brighton for a good day out (and who enjoyed a flirtation with the journalist before he was killed), begins to ferret out the truth. Pinkie is trapped, the trap's jaws are closing, and his frenzied, paranoid attempts to escape make his plunge towards damnation ever steeper, ever surer.

GREENE, Henry Graham
1904-1991
British citizen
First job: journalist
Began writing: aged 11; first
publication (poems) 1925
Other details: worked as
travel writer and film critic
in the 1930s; sued
(successfully) by Shirley
Temple for writing a review
regarded as libellous;
worked for the British
Foreign Office in the Second
World War.

Greene divided his fiction into two kinds: 'novels' and 'entertainments'. *Brighton Rock* is an 'entertainment'.

In every Greene story, the main character is trapped. The trap can be physical: a manhunt closing in. Or it can be psychological: the character's mind collapsing under the pressure of guilt or despair. In many stories both kinds of trap apply.

As each book proceeds, Greene shows the jaws of the trap remorselessly closing. Some characters writhe about, trying to free themselves. Others give in to fate. But all are equally doomed, and Greene details their plight as methodically, as unemotionally, as if he were a scientist writing notes.

Greene was a Roman Catholic, and so are many of his characters. But belief brings them little comfort. Pinkie, in *Brighton Rock*, is typical. He was once an altar-boy, but has long abandoned church-going. None the less, rags of faith hang in his mind like living things, filling him with a superstitious panic which (literally) crazes him. Like all Greene's characters, he gets no comfort from religion: it is just one more burden on an already crippled soul.

In Greene's 'novels', heavyweight themes like this have hypnotic power. Guilt attacks the characters wherever and whatever they are: they all really inhabit the same place, the chilly psychological hell one critic nicknamed 'Greeneland'.

The 'entertainments' are never quite so bleak. They are thrillers with Greeneish tinges. *Stamboul Train* describes a manhunt on the Orient Express, from the victim's point of view. *The Third Man* is about a man searching for his one-time best friend, now a drugs-dealer in war-ruined Vienna. The background of *Brighton Rock* is razor-gang violence in a gaudy, rundown 1930s seaside resort.

Greene's dialogue is fast, his plots are exciting, his characters are viciously compulsive. His dark view of humanity permeates each story, insidious as nerve-gas: you don't know it's there till its work is done. TV offers us a remorseless diet of good-and-evil contests, wrong-rightings, man-hunts. Compared to Greene's work they are junk food masquerading as a banquet.

OTHER GREENE 'ENTERTAINMENTS'
Stamboul Train
The Third Man
Our Man in Havana
The Ministry of Fear
Loser Takes All

GREENE NOVELS
The Power and the Glory
The Heart of the Matter
The End of the Affair
The Quiet American
The Human Factor

TRY THESE
David Dodge, *The Lights of Skaro*
Eric Ambler, *The Mask of Dimitrios/Coffin for Dimitrios*
Paul Theroux, *The Mosquito Coast*
Frederic Raphael, *Lindmann*

See also
Atwood, Crime and Thrillers, Golding, Highsmith, le Carré, Leonard

" Very faintly from the room above came the sound of coughing. Brewer said, 'She's woke up. I got to go and see her.'
'You stay here,' the Boy said, 'and talk.'
'She'll want turning.'
'When we've finished, you can go.'
Cough, cough, cough: it was like a machine trying to start and failing. Brewer said desperately, 'Be human. She won't know where I've got to. I'll only be a minute.'
'You don't need to be longer than a minute here,' the Boy said. 'All we want's what's due to us. Twenty pounds.'
'I haven't got it in the house. Honest I haven't.'
'That's too bad for you.' The Boy drew off his right glove. "

THOMAS HARDY
FAR FROM THE MADDING CROWD (1874)

● ● ● ● ● ● ● ● ● ● ● ● ● ● ● ●

THE STORY

Gabriel Oak, an impoverished farmer, works as a shepherd for Bathsheba Everdene, and loves her. Bathsheba is in love with the dashing Sergeant Troy, who marries her and then deserts her. Believing him dead, Bathsheba marries Farmer Boldwood. Troy then comes back, and events move to a climax – and to the final untangling of the knot of feelings between Bathsheba, Oak and Boldwood.

> HARDY, Thomas
> 1840-1928
> British citizen
> First job: architect
> Began writing: 1858
> Other details: gave up novels for poetry in 1897, and made a second (even more powerful) reputation as a poet.

OTHER HARDY NOVELS

The Mayor of Casterbridge
The Trumpet-Major
Under the Greenwood Tree (lighter)
Tess of the D'Urbervilles (grimmer)

TRY THESE

George Eliot, *Adam Bede*
D.H. Lawrence, *The Rainbow*
L.P. Hartley, *The Go-Between*
Nathaniel Hawthorne, *The Scarlet Letter*
François Mauriac, *The Nest of Vipers*

See also
Brontë, Dickens, Fowles

Hardy was brought up in rural Dorset, and recreated it in his novels as the fictional county 'Wessex'. Traditional country ways are crucial to his work. Farmers, herdsmen, carters and local tradespeople are central characters. Human life moves in step with the seasons, the needs of the land and of animals. Hardy sees Nature's ebb and flow as a living force, healing or destructive, but not to be challenged.

For all Hardy's feeling for rural tradition, in other ways he was a 'new' thinker. He was an atheist, a political radical, a supporter of Darwin. Although he was not known for generosity to women in his domestic life, he believed (long before such views were fashionable) that women and men had similar intellectual capacity and emotional needs of equal importance. Even his love of country ways was by no means uncritical. When he describes men's unheeding cruelty to women – something he does frequently – his prose seethes with contempt, and one scene in particular, when a husband auctions his wife at the start of *The Mayor of Casterbridge*, is written with a fury unmatched in all his other work.

Hardy was brought up on Shakespeare and the Bible, and as a young man read Aeschylus and Sophocles. This affected his own writing style. His English is grand and ceremonial, or (in scenes of rustic jollity) breaks into a kind of Shakespearean clown-speak. He shared with Greek tragedy the ideas that human affairs are controlled by uncaring, implacable destiny, and that however much we wriggle, we are hooked.

But although pessimism plays an essential part in Hardy's books, he is seldom depressing to read. There are two reasons. First is his delight in even the smallest details of rural life. Church musicians puffing through hymns by candlelight, a horse being harnessed, chitchat in a pub, cobblestones being laid – all are described with such affection that the writing almost glows. The second reason is Hardy's sympathy with his characters. He tells every moment of their moods, every flash of feeling or fantasy. He is particularly good at men, showing the whole range from macho strutters to prototype 1990s 'New Men', in touch with their feelings and able to confront their own and others' emotions unabashed. Hardy's granite style gives his books power and weight; his dazzling attention to the minutest aspects of people and countryside gives them unique appeal.

• • • • • • • • • • • • • • • • • • • •

66 Gabriel's nose was greeted by an atmosphere laden with the sweet smell of new malt. The conversation ... immediately ceased, and everyone ocularly criticized him to the degree expressed by contracting the flesh of their foreheads and looking at him with narrowed eyelids, as if he had been a light too strong for their sight. Several exclaimed meditatively, after this operation had been completed: –

'Oh, 'tis the new shepherd, 'a b'lieve.'

'We thought we heard a hand pawing about the door for the bobbin, but weren't sure 'twere not a dead leaf blowed across,' said another. 'Come in, shepherd; sure ye be welcome, though we don't know your name.'

'Gabriel Oak, that's my name, neighbours.'

The ancient maltster sitting in the midst turned at this, his turning being the turning of a rusty crane.

'That's never Gable Oak's grandson over at Norcomb – never!' he said, as a formula expressive of surprise, which nobody was supposed to take literally.

'My father and my grandfather were old men of the name of Gabriel,' said the shepherd placidly.

'Thought I'd know the man's face ... thought I did! And where be ye trading o't to now, shepherd?'

'I'm thinking of biding here,' said Mr Oak. 99

JOSEPH HELLER
CATCH-22 (1961)

● ● ● ● ● ● ● ● ● ● ● ● ● ● ●

'There was only one catch ... and that was Catch-22.'

'If you're sane enough to want to get out, you're sane enough to fly.'

━━ ━━ ━━ ━━ ━━ ━━ ━━

THE STORY
During the Second World War, the lives of US airmen on the Mediterranean island of Pianosa are constantly at risk, not from Germans or Italians, but from their own lunatic High Command. One by one, the young men fly, joke and die. Yossarian watches like an appalled outsider caught up in a massacre. The more crazily he behaves, the saner, more sensible he seems.

HELLER, Joseph
Born 1923
US citizen
First job: university teacher
Began writing: 1950s
Other details: suffered from near-fatal illness in 1980s, and wrote a savage book (*No Laughing Matter*) about his feelings and life in hospital.

TRY THESE
Richard Hooker, *M*A*S*H*
Leslie Thomas, *The Virgin Soldiers*
Len Deighton, *Bomber*
Herman Wouk, *The Caine Mutiny*
Peter George, *Red Alert*

For politicians and other non-combatants, the problem in a war is justifying what's going on. It has to seem necessary, glorious, heroic, even magnificent. For people doing the actual fighting, the problem is usually very much simpler: surviving.

This is Heller's view, and he shares it with hundreds of ordinary soldiers since wars began. Men and women at the battle-front often complain that those in charge are idiots, and that no one at home truly understands what a lunatic shambles war actually is. Most fighters are ordinary people, trapped by horrific events, and anxious only to do what they have to do and reach home unharmed.

Another common feeling, brilliantly used by Heller, is that war has no logic. It is like a vicious dream. Things keep happening, time after time, or break off in the middle and are never seen again. Logic is replaced by blur. Because anything is possible, nothing is surprising – and at the same time, everything is surprising. The only way to cope is to stick it out until the nightmare is over, you wake up and what passes for sanity rules again.

Heller makes bitter, dazzling farce of all this - you'll laugh till you die. In *Catch-22* everyone in authority is a gung-ho, bumbling fool, lethal with other people's lives. The 'lower ranks' are young airmen, flying terrifying bombing-missions over enemy targets, and trying to make the rest of their lives as normal, as boring, as they can.

Yossarian, the book's main character, watches with a kind of numb amazement.

It's as if he's in the story, but still can't believe a word of it. His name, in Spanish, means 'I know nothing', and he spends the book trying to puzzle out the point of his own and everyone else's existence – a doomed task, since that existence has no point.

All this could be unreadably preachy and symbolic. But Heller is a comedian, not a parson. The book offers a stomach-churning diet of human flesh: sliced, torn, charred, exploded. Heller's descriptions spare us none of it. But his prose is also rich in wisecracks, one-liners and the upside-down, inside-out logic which is his speciality. His approach to war is like that in the film and TV series *M*A*S*H* – but fiercer and funnier. When *Catch-22* came out, critics called it 'mind-spinning, comic, macabre, knockabout, nightmarish, ironic, bawdy, a roller-coaster' – and those were the ones who minced their words.

ANTI-WAR BOOKS

Stephen Crane, *The Red Badge of Courage*

Erich Maria Remarque, *All Quiet on the Western Front*

Norman Mailer, *The Naked and the Dead*

Jaroslav Hasek, *The Good Soldier Svejk*

Mario Vargas Llosa, *The City and the Dogs/The Time of the Hero*

OTHER HELLER BOOKS
God Knows
Something Happened
Good As Gold

See also
Atwood, Irving, Vonnegut

● ● ● ● ● ● ● ● ● ● ● ● ● ● ● ● ●

66 The chaplain was reeling with confusion. 'But you aren't authorized to censor letters, are you?'

'Of course not,' Corporal Whitcomb answered. 'Only officers are ever authorized to do that. I censored in your name.'

'But I'm not authorized to censor letters either. Am I?'

'I took care of that for you, too,' Corporal Whitcomb assured him. 'I signed someone else's name for you.'

'Isn't that forgery?'

'Oh, don't worry about that. The only one who might complain in a case of forgery is the person whose name you forged, and I looked out for your interests by picking a dead man. I used Washington Irving's name.' 99

GEORGETTE HEYER

COTILLION (1953)

● ● ● ● ● ● ● ● ● ● ● ● ● ● ● ●

THE STORY

Kitty Charing is brought up by her uncle, a miser and misanthrope. She learns social graces, and finds out how people behave, from romantic poetry and novels. When she reaches the age for marriage, Uncle Matthew invites all his nephews to propose to her, saying that he will leave all his money to the successful suitor. Will it be prosy Hugh, dogged but dim Dolphinton, romantic Jack or fashionable Freddy? Kitty goes to London before the problem is resolved – and her French cousin Camille enters the reckoning. Good-hearted girl that she is, Kitty has other people's love-affairs to help along, as well as resolving her own predicament. There is so much to do ...

HEYER, Georgette
1902-1974
British citizen
Began writing: 1920s
Other details: wife of a leading lawyer, and lived a society existence quite separate from her writing.

TRY THESE

Jane Austen, *Mansfield Park*
Sharon Walsh, *The Rose Domino*
Clare Darcy, *Eugenia*

See also
Austen, Romance of the Past, Trollope

cotillion dance designed for people in gorgeous, formal clothes: a series of elaborate steps, figures and ceremonial, in which the dancers keep changing partners, coming back to one another, separating, coming back ...

Heyer's novels provide unfailing pleasure. She is one of a handful of authors whose works are so beloved that readers become addicts, re-reading them year after year with undiminished joy. The books are high romance, set in Regency times (the 1810s, the period of Jane Austen's novels). They are light-hearted tales of young people falling in and out of love, against a background of dances, card-parties, picnics and expeditions from such fashionable spots as Bath or Brighton.

As well as the central romance, each novel contains other plot-ingredients – smugglers, highwaymen, pirates – and there is usually a secret to uncover or a mystery to solve. Many stories involve people hiding their true identities or natures. Heyer spends the first half of the book deliciously tangling all these plot-strands, and the second half untangling them.

But high-spirited plotting, for most readers, is not the main pleasure of her work: it is more her wonderful eye and ear for the detail of Regency society. She crammed dozens of notebooks with research on every aspect of early-nineteenth-century high life: clothes, food, make-up, the games people played, the books they read, their manners, gossip and above all their slang. She became so expert in all this that when she wrote she was like a virtuoso musician playing a concerto: you knew in your heart that everything came from hours of back-breaking hard work, but the result still seemed effortless, as natural as breathing.

The high comedy of human life could hardly have a better setting than the self-obsessed Regency period: extravagant, fun-loving, artificial and absurd. Heyer takes full advantage of this – and then trumps it by showing true human feelings, true emotions, underneath her characters' façades. Her books may be light-hearted froth, but the froth is expertly prepared and unfailingly delicious.

OTHER HEYER BOOKS
Heyer wrote some thirty Regency romances, including *Powder and Patch*, *Friday's Child*, *Regency Buck*, *These Old Shades*, *The Grand Sophy* and *The Nonesuch*. She also wrote historical novels (including *An Infamous Army*, reconstructing the Battle of Waterloo), and modern detective stories including *Envious Casca* and *They Found Him Dead*.

66 'Quite a romance, Frederick,' said his lordship, drawing out his snuff-box again.

'No, no!' disclaimed his blushing son. He added hurriedly: 'What I mean is, I shouldn't put it like that, myself!'

Lord Legerwood dipped his forefinger and thumb into the box, shook away all but a minute pinch of snuff and held this to one nostril. 'It distresses me to reflect that you have been labouring under the pangs of what you believed to be a hopeless passion, and that I remained in ignorance of it,' he observed. 'I must be a most unnatural parent. You must try to forgive me, Frederick.'

Thrown into acute discomfort, Freddy stuttered, 'N-never thought of such a th-thing, sir! That is – n-not as bad as that! Always fond of Kit, of course!'

Lord Legerwood, a sportsman and a gentleman, abandoned the pursuit of unworthy game, shut his snuffbox with a snap, restored it to his pocket, and said in quite another voice: 'In Dun Territory, Freddy?'

'No!' declared his unhappy son.

'Don't be a fool, boy! If you've steered your barque off Point Non-Plus, come to me for a tow, not to a chancy heiress!' 99

PATRICIA HIGHSMITH
RIPLEY'S GAME (1974)

●　●　●　●　●　●　●　●　●　●　●　●　●　●

THE STORY
Ripley is approached by an old acquaintance, Reeves. Two Italian Mafia 'families' are encroaching on Reeves' territory in Hamburg, and Reeves thinks that if one member of each family is mysteriously murdered, each will suspect the others and they will be so busy squabbling that they will leave him and his operation in peace. How, though, should the murders be committed? Ripley suggests persuading an innocent, ordinary man, an outsider, to commit the crimes. He offers to find such a man, and deliver him to Reeves. From that moment, for Jonathan Trevanny, frame-maker, no hope is left.

HIGHSMITH, (Mary) Patricia
Born 1921
US citizen
Began writing: early teens;
first published book 1950
Other details: decided to
become a professional
writer after editing the
school magazine; also
known as a painter and
sculptor.

OTHER 'RIPLEY' BOOKS
The Talented Mr Ripley
Ripley Underground
The Boy Who Followed Ripley
Ripley Under Water

At some stage in their lives, almost everyone in the Western world must have sat down to write a school essay entitled 'What I did on my holidays'. One's heart goes out to the unfortunate teacher, wading through pages of dutiful accounts of non-events – 'We went to the station. The train was late. We got into our carriage' – told in the same monotonous, flat prose.

Highsmith takes that same uneventful prose and turns it into chilling art. Her people get up, brush their teeth, go shopping, dig the garden, dust the furniture, walk the dog. Their lives are described in almost fussy detail. There seems to be no variety of pace; there seem to be no climaxes. And yet Highsmith books are compulsive: they create heart-thudding excitement, demand to be read at a sitting.

The reason is that Highsmith's characters are not ordinary people, but deranged. Some are psychopaths, others are driven insane as the book proceeds. Every novel involves someone who has killed, or who is about to kill. You know this before you start – and so, very often, does the character. Thus, the toneless, monotonous record of cooking breakfast, practising music, changing library books, buying arsenic is precisely not ordinary. It is an inexorable account of the progress towards a crime. When the murder happens (usually involving something perfectly domestic, such as a hammer, a lump of wood, a pair of scissors), it is described in the same unblinking way. The whole thing is as unemotional as a law-court confession, as clinical as a psychologist's case-study – and it has the same inescapable, icy pull.

Each of Highsmith's Ripley books is self-contained, but they all use the same basic cast: Tom Ripley, a charming US psychopath, his wife Héloïse and their cook-housekeeper Madame Annette. Ripley lives in a small French village. He is apparently a rich idler, an amateur painter and musician. But he earns his money by murder: no more than one or two a year, each committed anonymously, clinically, and far away from home. If things become 'messy' – for example, when innocent outsiders are unexpectedly involved – Ripley is forced to equally 'messy' action to sort things out, before going home to his beloved wife and house, as serene as if he'd just been on the 'little business trip' he claims.

OTHER HIGHSMITH NOVELS
A Dog's Ransom
The Cry of the Owl
This Sweet Sickness
The Tremor of Forgery

TRY THESE
Julian Symonds, *The Man Who Killed Himself*
Georges Simenon, *The Hatter's Ghosts*
Celia Fremlin, *Appointment with Yesterday*

See also
Crime and Thrillers, Dexter, Greene, Leonard, Paretsky, Simenon

● ● ● ● ● ● ● ● ● ● ● ● ● ● ● ●

❝ 'What a beautiful place!' Jonathan said.

Tom nodded and smiled. 'A wedding present from my wife's parents, mainly. And every time I arrive lately, I'm delighted to see that it's still standing. Please come in!'

Tom had a key for the front door, too. 'Not used to locking up,' Tom said. 'Usually my housekeeper's here.'

Jonathan walked into a wide foyer paved with white marble, then into a square living-room – two rugs, a big fireplace, a comfortable-looking yellow satin sofa. And a harpsichord stood beside French windows. The furniture was all good, Jonathan saw, and it was well cared for.

'Take off your mac,' Tom said. For the moment, he felt relieved – Belle Ombre was quiet, and he hadn't seen anything out of the ordinary in the village. He went to the hall table and took his Luger from the drawer. ❞

ANTHONY HOPE

THE PRISONER OF ZENDA (1894)

● ● ● ● ● ● ● ● ● ● ● ● ● ● ● ●

THE STORY

Rudolf Rassendyll, an English gentleman, is visiting Ruritania. It is the day before the coronation of his namesake Rudolf. The future king is captured and imprisoned in Zenda Castle by Rupert of Hentzau, henchman of the king's wicked brother, Michael, who covets his throne. A party of loyalists realizes that Rassendyll is the exact double of King Rudolf, and persuades him to take the king's place at the coronation. All Rudolf then has to do is break into Zenda, rescue the king and place him on the throne. One complication remains: Princess Flavia, King Rudolf's fiancée, has fallen in love with Englishman Rudolf, and doesn't yet know the truth of his identity ...

HOPE, Anthony
1863-1933
Real name: Anthony Hope Hawkins
British citizen
First job: lawyer
Began writing: 1890s
Other details: worked for Ministry of Information during First World War, feeding news to the papers; knighted not for novels but for this 'service to King and Country'.

See also

Dunnett, Fantasy and Horror, Romance of the Past, Stevenson

Before fantasy was invented, what did people read for adventure? One answer is books like this. *The Prisoner of Zenda* has all the ingredients of fantasy except magic. It is set in an imaginary country, Ruritania. There is a struggle between good and evil. The main character is no superhero, but an ordinary person forced to heroism by events. In every chapter there are plots, betrayals and skin-of-the-teeth escapes, and the whole thing floats on jokey dialogue – the worse things get, the sharper the one-liners.

Stories like this were hugely popular in early films. (*The Prisoner of Zenda* itself has been filmed half a dozen times.) Heroes were handsome, athletic and sexy. Villains were brooding, sneering and sexy. Heroines were beautiful, and in constant peril. The settings were castles, palaces, romantic inns and leafy forests (ideal to hunt in, or be hunted).

In all these stories, there was at least one sword-fight between the hero and the villain. Often, they duelled in the great hall of a castle. They fought up and down flights of huge stone stairs. As well as with swords they fought with cloaks, blazing torches, logs from the fire. Eventually the hero escaped by stunning his opponent, running to the battlements and diving, perfectly, hundreds of feet to the moat below.

Nowadays film versions of these stories are more often sent up than played straight. Stunts rule; the heroes are like Action Men, and the heroines like Barbie dolls. The books of such yarns, by contrast, pulse with action and fizz **with** wit. They force us to imagine the spectacle for ourselves, and this – except for literary couch potatoes – is what gives them life.

So-called 'interactive' novels (where you help the story along as you read) were claimed as an invention of the 1980s. In fact their equivalent had already existed for a century. In Hope's time they were called 'page-turners': tongue-in-cheek, escapist romps – and *The Prisoner of Zenda* was one of the best.

OTHER HOPE BOOKS
Rupert of Hentzau (sequel to *The Prisoner of Zenda*. Rudolf Rassendyll once again stars, rescuing Flavia from more Hentzau dastardliness. Major surprise kept, like a time-bomb, till the very end.)
Sophie of Kravonia
Tristram of Blent
Lucinda

TRY THESE
Rafael Sabatini, *Captain Blood*
Baroness Orczy, *The Scarlet Pimpernel*
Alexandre Dumas, *The Three Musketeers*

"

'Get off your horse,' I cried, 'And fight like a man.' 'Before a lady!' said he, pointing to the girl. 'Fie, your Majesty!'

Then in my rage, hardly knowing what I did, I rushed at him. I seized the bridle and I struck at him. He parried and thrust at me. I fell back a pace and rushed in at him again; and this time I reached his face and laid his cheek open, and darted back before he could strike me ...

There came a shout from behind us, and, looking round, I saw just at the turn of the avenue a man on a horse. He was riding hard, and he carried a revolver in his hand. It was Fritz von Tarlenheim, my faithful friend. Rupert saw him, and knew that the game was up. He checked his rush at me and flung his leg over the saddle, but yet just for a moment he waited. Leaning forward, he tossed the hair off his forehead and smiled, and said,

'Au revoir, Rudolf Rassendyll!'

Then, with his cheek streaming blood, but his lips laughing and his body swaying with ease and grace, he bowed to me ... clapped his heels hard in the horse's belly, and rode away at a gallop.

"

JOHN IRVING
THE WORLD ACCORDING TO GARP (1976)

●●●●●●●●●●●●●●●●

THE STORY

Garp's childhood is dominated by his surroundings (a tough private school), by his smallness (alleviated only when he learns to wrestle) and by his mother (a feminist who becomes a national guru). He goes to college, becomes a writer, marries a childhood friend and has children on whom he dotes. But, Irving explains, 'in the world according to Garp, we are all terminal cases', moving inexorably towards our deaths. To Garp's horror he finds that his writing only flowers when things go wrong in his personal life, that inspiration depends on terrible things happening to those he loves. He is trapped in an (unspoken) compact with the Devil, and the more he struggles the worse things get.

IRVING, John
Born 1942
US citizen
First job: university teacher (English)
Began writing: 1960s
Other details: hobbies include wrestling.

OTHER IRVING NOVELS
The Hotel New Hampshire
The Cider-House Rules
A Prayer for Owen Meany

Irving's novels follow the advice always given to would-be fiction authors: 'Write about what you know.' His books are about people growing up, baffled by the mysteries of experience, but nevertheless plunging into it and, by adding their own individual quirkiness, making it even more bizarre. Such feelings must be common to everyone. But when Irving describes them, he adds obsessions of his own – performing bears, Vienna, wrestling, old wooden buildings – and makes each book unique.

Garp begins with its hero's bizarre conception – his mother a nurse who despises emotion, his father a dead soldier – and moves on to describe his even odder childhood and adolescence. As in all Irving's novels, this 'growing-up' section is dazzling: he superbly catches the way hunger for experience, for understanding, is an all-consuming force in adolescence, and the way would-be sophistication usually ends in a pratfall.

Garp's childhood home is unusual, to say the least, and his friends are freakish. This, too, is par for Irving's course. Home in *Garp* is a rambling private school; in *The Hotel New Hampshire* it is a deserted hotel, in *The Cider-House Rules* an orphanage-cum-abortion-clinic. Garp's friends include an ex-footballer who has changed sex and a group of feminists who have cut out their tongues in protest against man's inhumanity to woman. The cast of *The Hotel New Hampshire* includes a performing bear and a group of terrorists hell-bent on taking over not the world but the Vienna State

Opera. The hero's father-figure in *The Cider-House Rules* is a saintly ether-addict.

Irving's books are continuously, irrepressibly surprising. But their oddness is not just for show. He believes that human life is painful as well as farcical, and that we stumble through it with no one to guide us, and no helpers along the road except (if we are lucky) our lovers and our friends. Human beings cause all mortal misery – but we are also each other's only hope. This harsh lesson is the one all Irving's heroes must learn – and in Garp's case the process is particularly painful, because he is also trying, as a writer to find some way to exorcize the grimness of the human condition by putting it in print.

TRY THESE

Russell Hoban, *Turtle Diary*

Philip Roth, *Portnoy's Complaint*

Robertson Davies, *What's Bred in the Bone* (second novel of the 'Cornish' trilogy)

Richard Brautigan, *Trout Fishing in America*

Joseph Heller, *Something Happened*

See also

Carey, Grass, Jolley, Heller

> In Garp's dream, he and Duncan had been riding on an airplane. Duncan had to go to the bathroom. Garp pointed down the aisle; there were doors down there, a small kitchen, the pilot's cabin, the lavatory. Duncan wanted to be taken there, to be shown which door, but Garp was cross with him.
>
> 'You're ten years old, Duncan,' Garp said. 'You can read. Or ask the stewardess.'
>
> ... Moodily, the child walked down the aisle toward the doors ... He got to the end of the aisle and glared back at Garp; Garp waved to him, impatiently. Duncan shrugged his shoulders, helplessly. Which door?
>
> Exasperated, Garp stood up. 'Try one!' he shouted down the aisle to Duncan ... Duncan was embarrassed and opened a door immediately – the one nearest to him. He gave a quick, surprised, but uncritical look back to his father before he seemed to be drawn through the door he'd opened ... The stewardess screamed. The plane gave a little dip in altitude, then corrected itself. Everyone looked out the windows ...

TOVE JANSSON
THE SUMMER BOOK (1972)

● ● ● ● ● ● ● ● ● ● ● ● ● ● ● ●

It is one of the features of adult human
beings that we can think about several
things at once. Adult brains are webbed
with thought, so much so that we find it
hard to accept simple things (smiles or sun-
sets, say) at their face value, without pondering about their wider 'meaning' for us
personally and for the human race at large.

Young children never do this. Neither
their brains nor their experience are suffi-
ciently developed. To adults, children seem
'innocent' and 'receptive'. As we watch
them discovering, we remember, fondly,
what it felt like to be so overwhelmed with
simple things.

Fondness is the tone of Jansson's brief,
beautiful novel. One of its two central characters is seven-year-old Sophia. Her mother
is dead, and Sophia is spending the summer
with her father and her grandmother on a
tiny island in the Gulf of Finland, a rock
just big enough for a house, garden and
mooring-place.

In this idyllic place, the only (rare) con-
tacts the family has with other people are
by boat. 'Reality' is stripped-down: sea,
sun, rock, plants, animals. Sophia is mature
beyond her years about some things: keeping the lamps filled; fishing; managing a
boat. But in every other way she is like a
blank notebook, receptive to all experience,
and she accepts things gladly, openly, as if
she were the first person in the world to
make each discovery, feel each emotion.
Jansson's descriptions, each time, are as
precise as poetry.

If this were a children's book, Sophia's

discoveries would be enough. (Jansson is a beloved children's writer, inventor of the amiable, magic Moomintrolls.) But *The Summer Book* is a novel for adults, and Grandmother, the second main character, is vital to its success. In her long life, Grandmother has thought most of the thoughts, experienced most of the joys and sorrows life has to offer. Her body is beginning to fail, and she spends much of her time managing it as one might control an unruly pet. But her mind is pin-sharp, so that she can strip away layers of memory and experience and focus exactly on whatever is to hand. This ability to concentrate on the essential is like Sophia's – except that Grandmother's experience allows her a subtler, more lateral view of reality, which Jansson contrasts poignantly with Sophia's naive response.

The Summer Book's other constant quality is radiance. James Joyce once wrote of 'epiphanies': small moments of joy or understanding in ordinary life which flood our souls. These are what Jansson deals in, not sentimentally but with sharpness and purity: vision exactly matched by style.

●●●●●●●●●●●●●●●●●●●●●●

66 'I can dive,' Sophia said. 'Do you know what it feels like when you dive?'

'Of course I do,' her grandmother said. 'You let go of everything and get ready and just dive. You can feel the seaweed against your legs. It's brown, and the water's clear, lighter towards the top, with lots of bubbles. And you glide. You hold your breath and glide and turn and come up, let yourself rise and breathe out. And then you float. Just float.'

'And all the time with your eyes open,' Sophia said.

'Naturally. People don't dive with their eyes shut.'

'Do you believe I can dive without me showing you?' the child asked.

'Yes of course,' Grandmother said. 'Now get dressed. We can get back before he wakes up.'

The first weariness came closer. When we get home, she thought, when we get back I think I'll take a little nap. And I must remember to tell him this child is still afraid of deep water. 99

JEROME K. JEROME
THREE MEN IN A BOAT (1889)

● ● ● ● ● ● ● ● ● ● ● ● ● ● ●

THE STORY

J. claims that his book is an
instruction manual on how to spend
a week boating on the Thames. Half
of it describes the tussles he, Harris
and George have with nature,
inanimate objects, boatyard-owners,
lock-keepers, landlords and anglers.
The rest is J.'s outpourings about
the history and landscape of the
places they pass: patriotic, romantic,
starry-eyed, and well over the top.

JEROME, Jerome Klapka
1859-1927
British citizen
First jobs: railway clerk;
teacher; reporter
Began writing: 1880s
Other details: once acted in
a *Hamlet* sliced down to 45
minutes for popular
consumption, and consisting
mainly of swordfights.

OTHER JEROME BOOKS

Three Men on the Bummel (sequel:
    cycling in Germany)
Diary of a Pilgrimage
Idle Thoughts of an Idle Fellow
My Life and Times (humorous
    autobiography)

The 'heroes' of *Three Men in a Boat* are
three of the most unremarkable people you
could ever hope to find: George, Harris
and J. (we never hear J.'s full name). There
is also the dog, Montmorency, whose idea
of heaven is fourteen fights before dinner,
and thirteen after. The book is a blow-by-
blow account of their rowing-trip up the
Thames from London to Oxford: a popular
holiday of young Londoners in the 1880s,
though never quite like this.

In *The Wind in the Willows*, also involving the River Thames, Ratty says, 'There is
nothing, absolutely nothing, half so much
worth doing as simply messing about in
boats.' This is the spirit in which George,
Harris and J. set out on their journey. In
prospect, it all seems superbly simple: load
a boat with a few simple possessions, row
or haul it upriver during the day, and at
evening set up camp in some leafy glade
before repairing to the nearest hostelry for
an unpretentious but delightful supper.

Such is our heroes' dream – and everything conspires against it. Oars, ropes, tins
of meat, stoves and gladstone bags take on
malign characters of their own, creating an
escalation of chaos which is greatly to the
taste of the jeering motor-boat owners and
stone-throwing small boys who lie in wait
at every turn. The weather is foul. George
and Harris are convinced that J. is slack-
ing. J., sure that he is doing all the work,
agrees with Harris that George is out of
condition, and with George that Harris is
an ineffectual dreamer. Montmorency sits
and waits for cats.

The whole thing is gently, serenely silly, and, in true British-comedy style, George, Harris and J. are convinced that they – bachelor clerks in the heyday of the British Empire – are the apex of creation, the gleam in God's eye when he made the Universe. As for the readers, we are in the happy position of the yokels with motor-boats or boys with stones. We do none of the work, and have all the fun.

TRY THESE
George and Weedon Grossmith, *The Diary of a Nobody*
Stephen Leacock, *Literary Lapses*
Alan Coren, *Golfing for Cats*
James Thurber, *My World – and Welcome to It!*

See also
Adams, Wodehouse

● ● ● ● ● ● ● ● ● ● ● ● ● ● ● ●

❝ It was very cold when I got back into the boat after swimming, and in my hurry to get my shirt on, I accidentally jerked it into the water. It made me awfully wild, especially as George burst out laughing. I could not see anything to laugh at, and I told George so, and he only laughed the more. I never saw a man laugh so much. I quite lost my temper with him at last, and I pointed out to him what a drivelling maniac of an imbecile idiot he was; but he only roared the louder. And then, just as I was landing the shirt, I noticed that it was not my shirt at all but George's, which I had mistaken for mine; whereupon the humour of the thing struck me for the first time, and I began to laugh. And the more I looked from George's wet shirt to George, roaring with laughter, the more I was amused, and I laughed so much that I had to let the shirt fall back into the water again.

'Ar'n't you – you – going to get it out?' said George between his shrieks.

I could not answer him at all for a while, I was laughing so, but at last, between my peals, I managed to jerk out:

'It isn't my shirt – it's yours!'

I never saw a man's face change from lively to severe so suddenly in all my life before. **❞**

Elizabeth Jolley
Miss Peabody's Inheritance (1983)

● ● ● ● ● ● ● ● ● ● ● ● ● ● ● ● ● ●

THE STORY

Miss Peabody, a lonely Londoner with a bedridden mother, writes a fan-letter to the (Jolley-ish) Australian novelist Diana Hopewell. In reply, she gets a scene from Hopewell's novel-in-progress, about an eccentric headmistress touring Europe with her lover, a colleague and a lumpish sixteen-year-old pupil. The correspondence flourishes, until the bizarre events of the letters become more real to Miss Peabody than her own drab existence. She longs to enter Hopewell's extraordinary world for herself – and in a perfectly natural but quite unexpected way, she is given the chance to do just that.

JOLLEY, Elizabeth
Born 1923
Australian citizen
Other jobs: nurse; goose-farmer; 'flying domestic'; orchard-owner; travelling salesperson; teacher of creative writing in prisons, community centres and Institutes of Technology
Began writing: 1970s
Other details: born in Britain; brought up in a German-speaking household (father was Austrian); settled in Australia in 1959.

Jolley sets her books in Australia. However, her outback is not the actual outback, her suburbs are not actual suburbs, the houses and streets her people live in are no different from those in Wales or Arizona. The true location of her books is a mesmeric place where ordinariness is no more than a disguise, where obsession and fantasy rule.

Perhaps because of this constant exotic presence, the internal landscapes of Jolley's characters run riot in a similar way. The people take up bizarre sex, blackmail, embezzlement, murder, as casually and as matter-of-factly as one might develop an interest in philately or macramé.

In Jolley's hands, the collision between eccentricity and respectability is hilarious. Her books are funny not in set-piece fits and starts but continuously, as if she bubbles with merriment as she types each line. But because her characters are so gentle, and the odd things they do are simultaneously so liberating and so doomed – we know as we read that each book will end in tears – the over-riding mood of her work is sad and thoughtful. This sadness is never laid on; it seeps in unannounced. Jolley's writing style is – well, jolly. It is as if she asked herself each morning, 'What fun shall we have today?' She starts each story with a bizarre situation, explores it thoroughly and then moves smoothly to the next, like an athlete constantly setting herself new, small challenges. And the situations are bizarre. The heroine of *Palomino*, a doctor struck off for murdering a patient, falls in love with a stranger on an ocean voyage and takes her back home as a kind of pet, a souvenir. The heroine of *Foxybaby* tries to make an experimental film with a group of uncooperative adult students at a sinister summer-school-cum-slimming establishment deep in the outback. In *The Sugar Mother*, a pushy mother and her lumpish daughter literally move in on a lonely professor whose wife has set off on a year-long, world-wide lecture tour.

Starting-points like these read like subjects given to stimulate a writing class, with the instruction 'Do what you like with this'. Jolley follows that advice to the letter. She does exactly what she likes, deliciously unpredictable. She is like someone calmly telling tales of terrible events, who every so often cracks into cackles of sinister, sly laughter, instantly suppressed.

OTHER JOLLEY NOVELS
The Newspaper of Claremont Street
Milk and Honey
My Father's Moon
Cabin Fever

TRY THESE
Hilary Mantel, *Fludd*
Anita Brookner, *Look at Me*
Alison Lurie, *The Truth About Lorin Jones*
Mary Wesley, *The Vacillations of Poppy Carew*

See also
Carter, Irving, Morris, Tyler, Vargas Llosa, Winterson

● ● ● ● ● ● ● ● ● ● ● ● ● ● ● ● ●

❝ 'Turn,' Debbie says. 'Turn and turn and step but don't touch! Not yet!' She's laughing. 'It's disco Miss Thorne. It's disco!'
The girl is singing softly and dancing all round her.
'Come on Miss Thorne, Miss Arabella Thorne, I can teach you. I can teach you a lot of things. I can teach you what to do with your hands.'
... 'No thank you Debbie,' Miss Thorne replies quietly, looking down from her immense height. 'And now I think it is time for bed,' she looks at her watch. 'Good gracious! it's well after midnight. What about our Beauty Sleep? Part of the night is for sleep, especially for you young gels with examinations ahead. So goodnight Debbie, orf you go now, orf into bed!'
'Miss Thorne, I want to stay with you all night. Can I stay please?'
'I am afraid that's not possible Debbie. I do however completely understand your feelings'... ❞

John le Carré
A Perfect Spy (1986)

●●●●●●●●●●●●●●●●

THE STORY

Hiding out in a tatty British seaside resort, Magnus Pym writes the story of his life. He is a handsome, popular diplomat, with a wife and adoring son – and, throughout his adult life, he has also been an agent. He traces the influences which made him what he is – his schooldays, his friendships, his longing to achieve conventional English respectability despite the fact that his father is a conman. He realizes that he has spent his life trying to seduce the world, and that the espionage circus has used his need for acceptance to seduce him. He is hollow, an actor who can no longer believe in the part he plays. How he faces this is the subject of the book.

LE CARRÉ, John
Born 1931
Real name: David John
Moore Cornwell
British citizen
First jobs: language teacher;
diplomat
Began writing: early 1960s
Other details: taught at Eton,
and first book was
Call for the Dead, a murder
mystery set in an English
boarding school.

See also
Crime and Thrillers, Greene

Spy novels were particularly popular in the years between the end of the Second World War and the end of the Cold War – and the reason is plain. They deal with the balance between loyalty and treachery, and in a war situation (especially, perhaps, in the Cold War, where hostilities are verbal rather than physical) few people doubted that there was a moral gulf between Us (muddled but decent) and Them (ruthless and devious).

'Us-Good-Them-Bad' spy books are still being written. But even twenty years ago, their politics were beginning to seem old-fashioned. More thoughtful writers were suggesting that human affairs were more complicated than playground games. Issues of loyalty and treachery were not straightforward; the espionage world existed not in primary colours but in every imaginable shade of grey.

This enigmatic, claustrophobic world is le Carré's home territory. His spies are employed by specific countries, each with its own particular brand of politics: the UK, the former USSR, the US, former East Germany. But in fact the spies 'belong' to no real state at all. They are all members of the same unofficial espionage bureaucracy, what le Carré calls a 'circus' (in Britain, The Circus). The systems and methods of this bureaucracy are the same worldwide – and they are as labyrinthine, as secretive and as self-perpetuating as those of any other vast conglomerate.

In this stifling atmosphere, very little actually happens. A single 'operation' (saving an agent from being unmasked abroad, say, or eliminating a traitor in the Circus itself) may take a whole book to set up and complete. But the process of psychological discovery, peeling away the onion-layers of personality, is both unpredictable and compulsive. Le Carré's themes may seem undemonstrative, but his books are as exhilarating to read as any fast-action thriller.

'THE CIRCUS'

Le Carré's best-known books about 'The Circus' are a trilogy centring on the brilliant, enigmatic George Smiley. They are published separately, as *Tinker Tailor Soldier Spy*, *Smiley's People* and *The Honourable Schoolboy*, and in one volume as *The Quest for Karla*.

OTHER LE CARRÉ BOOKS
The Russia House
The Spy Who Came in from the Cold
A Small Town in Germany
The Little Drummer Girl

TRY THESE
Len Deighton, six-novel 'Bernard Samson' sequence (books can be read separately): *Berlin Game*, *Mexico Set*, *London Match*, *Spy Hook*, *Spy Line*, *Spy Sinker*
Andrew Taylor, *Blacklist*
Bryan Forbes, *Familiar Strangers*
Robert McCrum, *In the Secret State*

● ● ● ● ● ● ● ● ● ● ● ● ● ● ●

❝ He phoned Kate. No answer.
He phoned his wife. No answer.
He phoned Paddington and wrote down the times and places along the route of the sleeper from Paddington to Penzance via Reading.
For an hour he tried to sleep, then returned to his desk, pulled Langley's folder towards him and stared yet again at the eaten-out features of Herr Petz-Hampel-Zaworski, Pym's presumed controller, lately of Corfu. '... real name unknown ... query member Czech archaeological team visiting Egypt 1961 ... height 6ft., stoops, limps slightly with left leg ...'
He continued to stare at the photograph. The down-turned eyelids. The down-turned moustache. The twinkly eyes. The hidden Slav smile. Who the devil are you? Why do I recognize you when I never set eyes on you? ❞

ELMORE LEONARD
FREAKY DEAKY (1988)

● ● ● ● ● ● ● ● ● ● ● ● ● ● ●

freaky deaky 1960s dance craze, in which people jumped up and down with stiff, out-stretched arms and legs, like dolls thrown into the air by an explosion. Jive for 'wild'.

- - - - - - - - -

THE STORY

Skip and Robin were student revolutionaries at the time of Woodstock, and were jailed for dynamiting a Federal building. Now, eighteen years on, they set out to hunt down the man who betrayed them. They themselves are being hunted, by burned-out cop Chris Mankowski. The line-up is completed by boozy, brain-dead multi-millionaire Mr Woody, by Greta Wyatt (alias bit-part actress and dancer Ginger Jones), by Donnell (the cool dude who looks after Mr Woody) and by bags and bags of high explosive.

> LEONARD, Elmore
> **Born 1925**
> **US citizen**
> **First jobs: US navy;**
> **advertising**
> **Began writing: 1950s**
> **Other details: until he**
> **became a full-time novelist**
> **and screenwriter in 1967, his**
> **books were potboiler**
> **westerns. Basic rule: the**
> **more recent a Leonard book,**
> **the better.**

For centuries, the reading public has been fascinated by criminals. Eighteenth-century Londoners fought for copies of the *Autobiography* of the highwayman Jack Shepherd. In nineteenth-century Paris stories of kidnap and murder drew the crowds. In the US of the 1920s you could make a fortune by writing about floozies, speakeasies and gangsters with names like Scarface, Lefty and Bugsy. Our taste nowadays is for books about the big-city 'underclass': drug-pushers, hookers, muggers, winos and the innocents or not-so-innocents they prey on.

In most of these books, it has never really been the crimes themselves which fascinate. They are central to the plot, but in the telling they usually take second place to details of the criminals' daily lives. Jack Shepherd's fans created a fashion for dressing like him and talking 'his' slang. Thanks to film and TV, we are as familiar nowadays with the sleazy alleys, diners and apartments of US big cities as with our own back yards. Even small children know what 'punks' and 'graffiti' are; street-smartness is a quality admired throughout the world – and not just on the streets.

Street-smartness is as natural to Leonard's characters as breathing. They are born knowing how to hustle. Life is a lethal game, and you win by always having something to deal, always watching your back, and never showing mercy. In Leonard's world, the weakest always go to the wall: it is a manic, fast-forward version of Darwin's theory of evolution. Leonard's books are literally 'action-packed': a dozen things happen on every page, and if you skip so much as a sentence you may miss something vital. Cuts on TV happen nowadays roughly once every twelve seconds – and this, in prose, is how Leonard writes.

Above all, pace comes from dialogue. Everyone speaks a rapid, spatter-gun English which is Leonard's speciality. It is rap, or jive: the same basic pattern is ornamented, made personal, by every single character. Leonard's dialogue gives his books a unique kind of never-never-land feeling. He seems to be writing about gritty – very gritty – reality, but his stories are as fantastical as nightmares. Many of the best crime-writers (Chandler, Simenon, Wambaugh, McBain) do something similar. But if Leonard is in classy company, he still outsmarts it at every turn.

OTHER LEONARD BOOKS
Stick
Glitz
Bandits
Killshot
The Switch
Touch

TRY THESE
Chester Himes, *Cotton Comes to Harlem*
Joseph Wambaugh, *The Glitter Dome*
Richard Stark, *Slayground*
Colin Dunne, *Ratcatcher*

See also
Crime and Thrillers, Greene, Heller, Highsmith, Paretsky

● ● ● ● ● ● ● ● ● ● ● ● ● ● ● ●

> Booker was clutching the chair arms again, his body upright, telling Chris, 'Get that shit out from under me, man. Get it out, get it out of there!'
>
> Chris said, 'Somebody doesn't like you, Booker. Two sticks would've been plenty.'
>
> Booker said, 'Will you pull that shit out? Do it.'
>
> Chris sat back on his heels, looking up at Booker. 'I'm afraid we have a problem.'
>
> 'What problem. What you talking about?'
>
> 'See, most of the foam padding's been taken out. There's something in there that looks like an inflatable rubber cushion, fairly flat, laying on top of the dynamite.'
>
> 'So pull the shit out, man. You see it, pull it out.'
>
> 'Yeah, but what I don't see is what makes it go bang. It must be in the back part, where the cushion zips open.'
>
> 'Then open the motherfucker.'
>
> 'I can't, you're sitting on it.'

G. H. Morris
DOVES AND SILK HANDKERCHIEFS (1986)

● ● ● ● ● ● ● ● ● ● ● ● ● ● ● ●

THE STORY

This book of the 'Brightside' trilogy
centres on three members of the
family: indomitable Great-great-
grandmother, born in 1815 and still
going strong on the eve of the Great
War; Albert, willing to try anything
from socialism to the first reusable
condom in Yorkshire; and Lancaster,
who learns to fly as a child, and in
adulthood becomes a silent-film
pioneer. There are strikes and
lockouts; the Titanic hits an iceberg;
the First World War is fought – but
none of these events seem as
momentous to young Donald, the
narrator, as the saga of Sidall
Junkin's false teeth or Mr Brown's
explosive bags.

MORRIS, Gerald Harvey
Born 1939
British citizen
First jobs: pharmacist;
company director
Began writing: 1970s
Other details: founded his
own pharmaceutical
company, and ran it for 30
years. Became a full-time
writer after the success of
this trilogy.

THE 'BRIGHTSIDE' TRILOGY
Doves and Silk Handkerchiefs
Grandmother, Grandmother, Come
 and See
The Brightside Dinosaur

Doves and Silk Handkerchiefs is the first
book of the 'Brightside' trilogy, a lunatic,
wry family saga set in a Yorkshire mining
village between 1859 and 1950 – a mixture
of the magic realism in such books as
Vargas Llosa's *Aunt Julia and the
Scriptwriter* and sitcoms such as *Last of the
Summer Wine*. Each novel is self-contained,
but together they give a panorama of exotic
characters and bizarre events, as gaudy and
satisfying as a band parade.

To deal with serious matters first. Morris
describes the village and its life with almost
documentary grimness. He shows us a society inching its way from the filth and bustle
of the nineteenth-century Industrial Age to
the greater comfort but devastating political
and social uncertainty of the mid-twentieth
century. Details of mining life are all-
pervasive: the characters include 'pony-
boys' and 'checkweighmen', and background events include the stirrings of trade
unionism, and a stream of horrific accidents
and illnesses. Coal-dust hangs over the
books like a pall: it symbolizes the old
ways, so that every advance is like a lung-
ful of fresh air, an escape to cleanness and
wide blue sky.

This serious background is never
stressed, never dwelt on, but always there.
Even so, social documentary is not Morris'
main concern at all. His village is a place
crammed with stories, and the stories are
amazing. Children, equipped by a magician
with inflatable rubber suits, bounce and fly
like roly-poly cherubs. Parachutists float
from the sky wearing double-gusseted

French knickers. A horse gallops into the galleries of the mine and is lost for years, until its bones are found standing guard over a fossil dinosaur. When the dinosaur is placed in the village museum, it is brought back to life to the strains of Mozart's 'Prague' symphony on a fairground organ.

Donald Brightside, the story-teller, is innocent and gullible, the ideal curator for Morris' 'amazing-but-true' collection of characters and anecdotes. His beloved, Clarrie, wire-walks in a circus. Other characters include the five Gill brothers ('built like a brick shithouse and ... twice as nasty'), blind Squire Potterton the pheasant shooter, and Elyahou Tsiblitz, the Transylvanian rubber-goods salesman. Mixing realism and stand-up comedy is risky, but Morris manages it triumphantly. He is a magician, unpicking ordinary life and showing us wonders.

TRY THESE
Peter Tinniswood, *A Touch of Daniel*
Rony Robinson, *The Beano*
Keith Waterhouse, *Billy Liar*
David Nobbs, *A Bit of a Do*

See also
Carter, Durrell, Heller, Irving, Vargas Llosa

66 'Youngest first,' he said, kneeling on the seat and poking his head on its long neck over his backside, so that he could see out of the cab. 'Line up, line up.'

The women lined up the children in order of age, and ... in no time at all, Elyahou had half a dozen younger ones in rubber costume for the first time. Lion, tiger, sheep, horse and elephant were joyfully bouncing about the common while the fat child in the fat chicken could only succeed in rolling tamely about the grass. Some of the older ones took this as an opportunity to leave the line, deciding that a game of football with the unfortunate poultry was better even than the experience of dressing up ... My great-great-grandmother came down from a trip to the Roman wall just in time to see Lancaster yet again going up in the bee's outfit. Emily, who had not witnessed the flight of her son before ... slung her eyes heavenwards and shouted advisedly, 'Flap your arms, dear. Doggy-paddle' – as if she were advising him on how to swim. 99

V. S. NAIPAUL

A HOUSE FOR MR BISWAS (1961)

● ● ● ● ● ● ● ● ● ● ● ● ● ● ● ●

THE STORY
Mohun Biswas is haunted as a child by the fact that his father was a failure. As an adult he feels that this failure has transferred to him, and that everything he does is frustrated by circumstance (not to mention his wife's family). He tries to live a principled life, to bring up his children to be more successful than he is himself – and above all to live in a house of his own: a symbol that he has made his mark in the world.

NAIPAUL, Vidiadhar
Surajprasad
Born 1932
British citizen
First job: radio producer
Began to write: 1950s
Other details: traveller and
political commentator
(wrote *An Area of Darkness*
and *India: a Wounded
Civilisation*, about India, and
Among Believers, about
Islam).

OTHER NAIPAUL NOVELS
*The Suffrage of Elvira, Miguel
Street, The Mystic Masseur, The
Mimic Men* (all set on Trinidad)
The Enigma of Arrival

The chief setting of *A House for Mr Biswas* is Hanuman House, the many-roomed home of the Tulsi family. The Tulsis are shopkeepers, and they live above a general store the size of an aircraft hangar. The family centres on its women: the matriarch Mrs Tulsi and her half dozen daughters. Each time one of the daughters marries, her husband is taken into the house and becomes part of the family. At the time of the story there are over a dozen adults and two or three dozen children in Hanuman House, falling over each other, squabbling and watching each other like hawks to make sure that they, not their relatives, are treated to best advantage.

Mr Biswas, sucked into this ménage almost by accident, becomes one of the sons-in-law. But he has no talent for business. He has an artistic soul, and longs to express himself as a painter or a writer. He is a Brahmin, higher-caste than the rest of the family. His Tulsi relatives (including his wife) make no effort to understand or welcome him, and he makes no secret of his scorn for them and his determination to escape as soon as he can afford a house of his own. Unfortunately he has neither skills nor income, and is forced to work at the dead-end jobs the Tulsis find for him.

This situation is tragic and comic all at once, and Naipaul mingles the two modes throughout his book. Human relationships lead to comedy: sometimes slapstick, sometimes dark, but always satirical. Tragedy comes from the dilemma of Mr Biswas' own personality. He is a genius with no talent; he suffers the anguish of a creator but can make nothing. He is a failure as husband, son-in-law, father, estate manager, and even as sinner: his anger, lust, covetousness – all the deadly sins – are never significant, just enough to annoy his relatives and bring maximum suffering to himself. Like Naipaul's other novels and stories set on Trinidad, *A House for Mr Biswas* is something of an allegory. The Biswases and Tulsis are Indians, and feel set apart from the rest of the population. Mr Biswas' feelings of isolation and rejection symbolize this. But his anguish is not special to Hindus, to 1930s Trinidad, or to him alone. His misery is commonplace, and as we read about his predicament it is hard to know whether to laugh or cry.

TRY THESE
Shiva Naipaul, *Fireflies* (by V.S. Naipaul's brother, also set among the Indian community on Trinidad)
R.K. Narayan, *A Tiger for Malgudi*
Paul Theroux, *Fong and the Indians*
David Cook, *Sunrising*
Margaret Drabble, *The Garrick Year*

See also
Carey, Jolley, Tyler, Vargas Llosa

66 'Trapped!' Mr Biswas would say. 'You and your family have got me trapped in this hole.'

'Yes,' Shama would say. 'I suppose if it wasn't for my family you would have a grass roof over your head.'

'Family! Family! Put me in one poky little barrackroom and pay me twenty dollars a month. Don't talk to me about your family.'

'I tell you, if it wasn't for the children – '

And often, in the end, Mr Biswas would leave the house and go for a long night walk through the city, stopping at some empty shack of a café to eat a tin of salmon, trying to stifle the pain in his stomach and only making it worse; while below the weak electric bulb the sleepy-eyed Chinese shopkeeper picked and sucked his teeth, his slack, bare arms resting on a glasscase in which flies slept on stale cakes. 99

R. K. NARAYAN
THE PAINTER OF SIGNS (1976)

● ● ● ● ● ● ● ● ● ● ● ● ● ● ● ●

THE STORY

Raman, a moderately successful sign-painter, is contented with his lot until he falls in love with Daisy from the Family Planning Centre. Daisy is a fanatical supporter of the Gandhi government's 1970s policy of inducing peasant parents to reduce the size of their families by practising birth control – and she persuades Raman into a lunatic expedition into the countryside to convert minds, win hearts and distribute condoms. Raman is being dragged, only half unwillingly, into the twentieth century – and all the time, like an ever-present reminder of the Hindu certanties of India's past, his uncomplaining, elderly and devout aunt lives in his house and complicates his life.

> NARAYAN, Rasipuran
> Krishnaswami
> Born 1907
> Indian citizen
> First job: journalist
> Began writing (fiction): 1930s
> Other details: as a young man, worked briefly as a schoolteacher, and later had an even briefer, even less satisfying, flirtation with films: not his medium at all.

See also
Jansson, Naipaul

▬ ▬ ▬ ▬ ▬ ▬ ▬ ▬ ▬ ▬

Narayan's books are set in Malgudi, an imaginary small town in Southern India. In the distance are the Mempi Hills, where tigers may still roam. But the Malgudians seldom venture there. They are content with their own small universe: main street, river, school, shops, temple.

Geographical contentment, however, is not matched by serenity of soul. Narayan's characters feel ill-at-ease with themselves, sense a gulf between what they are and what they wish they were. They try to change their condition, to live up to their own ambitions – and their doomed efforts lead to bitter, gentle farce.

Usually, Narayan's characters long to shed their insignificance, to make some mark in the world. But they have no idea how to do it, and their schemes are bizarre. The hero of *The Financial Expert* is a money-lender whose longing to be a publisher leads him to finance the printing of a pornographic manuscript. In *The Guide* a conman sets up as a religious guru – and is embarrassed to find that he really has the authority he pretends. The hero of *The Man-Eater of Malgudi* is a crazed taxidermist, stuffing ever-larger animals until he over-reaches himself by planning to kill and mount the town's sacred elephant.

The second tragi-comic factor in a Narayan story is usually a close relationship: husband and wife, father and son, two friends, lovers. One of the pair is the dissatisfied hero of the story; the other is a kind of spectator, appalled at what's happening but unable to stop it. Often, one character is a devout Hindu and the other is not – allowing Narayan to balance old Indian ways (which stand for continuity and spiritual calm) and twentieth-century ideas (which stand for anarchy and uproar).

Narayan's novels are short (seldom more than 150 pages), and their casts are as small as their location: the teeming India of epic novels and films has no place here. In such a stripped-down style, the smallest events impact like bombs. The beginning of a love-affair, cataclysmic for one character, is a single hand-touch beside a river at evening. The collapse of a cherished relationship begins when one partner announces that she has bought a one-way ticket to Benares (where devout Hindus go to die). The novels are a parade of such 'ordinary' happenings, but Narayan's stylistic compression and self-restraint give them the power of poetry.

OTHER NARAYAN BOOKS
Mr Sampath
The Talkative Man
A Tiger for Malgudi
Lawley Road (short stories)
My Days (memoirs)

TRY THESE
Anita Desai, *The Clear Light of Day*
S.N. Ghose, *And Gazelles Leaping*
Kazuo Ishiguro, *An Artist of the Floating World*

> One evening he was at work in the back yard of his home, with the river flowing a few yards away. His aunt was away at the temple ... Raman had planed the eighteen-by-twelve board smoothly and put on the primary coat of paint, turned it towards the wall to save it from sand particles, and was rehearsing on a small pad the actual lettering to come. Over the short back wall, where sometimes the head of a goatherd would appear, appeared another head now – he became aware of it from a corner of his eye. He turned his back and went on with his work ... Hallucination? Yes, too common when one's mind was obsessed with a single figure. However, the sight thrilled him. He found it difficult to return to the word 'Nylon', which the bangle-seller wished to be emphasised on the sign-board. The danger nowadays was that he was likely to write 'Two Will Do – Limited Family Means ...' to every message; Ah! Daisy!

Sara Paretsky
Bitter Medicine (1987)

● ● ● ● ● ● ● ● ● ● ● ● ● ● ● ●

THE STORY
Warshawski helps a terrified
teenager, in emergency labour, to
the nearest private hospital. The
hospital is phoney, the girl dies, and
Warshawski sets out to find out how,
what and why. Lies, seduction and
mayhem lurk round every turn. The
only real questions are: which
hunky, rich smoothie can
Warshawski trust? And will the case
wreck her relationship with her
oldest, dearest (and hottest-
tempered) friend Dr Lotty Herschel?

MORE WARSHAWSKI BOOKS
Indemnity Only
Killing Orders
Toxic Shock
Guardian Angel

○ PARETSKY, Sara
○ Born 1947
○ US citizen
○ First jobs: secretary; sales
○ manager (insurance)
○ Began writing: 1980s
○ Other details: Chairwoman,
○ Sisters in Crime (cover name
○ for a group of US women
○ crime-writers).

CLASSIC PRIVATE EYE NOVELS
Dashiell Hammett, *The Maltese
    Falcon*
Raymond Chandler, *Farewell, My
    Lovely*
Ross Macdonald, *The Instant
    Enemy*

private eye (US slang): a detective who
    works for himself or herself, not
    attached to any police force. So
    called because the first-ever US
    detective agency, Pinkerton's,
    had the motto 'We Never Sleep',
    and used as its symbol a
    wide-open eye.

The first private eye stories were written
in the 1920s, and ever since private eyes
have topped the ratings in books, films
and TV series. For a few dollars a day,
plus expenses, they go where few police
detectives care to tread. They usually trust
no one and work alone. They sift the
moral garbage-heaps of crime and big
business. If there are skeletons in a family
cupboard, they prise them out. They are
good at picking locks, handy with guns,
and lethal with one-liners.

Ten years ago, Sara Paretsky had the
dazzling, simple idea of writing private-
eye novels not about a snappy-talking, no-
nonsense male but a snappy-talking, no-
nonsense female. V.I. ('Vic') Warshawski
is street-wise, brainy and stunningly beautiful. (Kathleen Turner played her on the
screen.)

Because no man ever believes what
Warshawki does for a living, she can bluff
her way into situations and extract confi-
dences as no mere male could ever do.
Then, when things turn tough, she outsmarts, out-talks, outbrawls every man in
sight. There's nothing feminist about this
(as there is in some other books starring
female private eyes). Warshawki is just

another working sleuth, using what personal strengths she has to do the job. The fact that those strengths are devastating is just her (and our) good luck.

Warshawki's 'patch' is Chicago, and her speciality (financial fraud) leads her into a world where every banker is on the make, every politician on the take, every corner crammed with gangsters, silly-rich bitches and the vultures who prey on them.

Warshawski narrates the books herself. She tells us everything: not just about the investigation, but what she eats, wears, dreams about, even how she jogs. She takes more showers in each book than most male sleuths do in their entire careers. Just as male detectives tend to have a weakness for long-legged blondes, so she collects rich, handsome men.

Paretsky's plots twist and barrel like roller-coaster rides. Her style is sleek and fast. If you like this sort of thing, and don't yet know these books, expect a treat.

MALE PRIVATE EYES

Almost as good as Paretsky: Benny Cooperman (in Howard Engels, *A City Called July*); Spenser (in Robert B. Parker, *Looking for Rachel Wallace*); Bernie Rhodenbarr (in Robert Block, *Burglars Can't Be Choosers*) – Rhodenbarr is a crime-solving burglar rather than a private eye, but his inventor all but outdoes Paretsky for plot and wit; Jimmy Jenner, an English private eye (in John Milne, *Daddy's Girl*).

FEMALE PRIVATE EYES

Almost as good as Paretsky: Sue Grafton's 'Kinsey Millhone' books. Each title begins with a letter of the alphabet: *A is for Alibi*; *B is for Burglar*, and so on. Recommended English private eyes: Cordelia Gray (in P.D. James' *An Unsuitable Job for a Woman*); Jemima Shore (in Antonia Fraser's *Quiet as a Nun*).

See also
Crime and Thrillers, Leonard

> It was time for whiskey, bath and bed. Near the entrance to the tollway I found a motel which even at this late hour was willing to provide me with all three. I took a double Black Label from the bar up to my room. By the time I'd finished soaking in the narrow tub I'd drunk all the whiskey. Practice makes perfect in these precision-timed exercises. I fell into bed and slept the perfect sleep of the honest laborer.

TERRY PRATCHETT
THE COLOUR OF MAGIC (1983)

●●●●●●●●●●●●●●●●

THE STORY
Rincewind is taking Twoflower on an expedition through Discworld. Twoflower is a tourist with enough gold to buy the universe, a picture-taking box and luggage with a temper of its own. Every pirate, troll, hoodlum, dragon-lord and drunk feels certain that Twoflower's gold is a burden to him, and that it would be a kindness to remove it. The Patrician of Ankh-Morpork wants Twoflower dead. Rincewind knows nothing of any of this. All he can tell is that Death is panting after him like an incompetent ferret, and that everyone is out to catch him and do unspeakable things to him.

> PRATCHETT, Terry
> **Born 1948**
> **British citizen**
> **First job: journalist**
> **Began writing: 1970s**
> **Other details: hobby (he says, warningly) is growing carnivorous plants.**

Jokes and fantasy don't often mix. Most fantasy novels are serious affairs involving quests, heroes, monsters, highly complicated magic and a vast amount of slicing, mashing and disembowelling.

Pratchett's books are different. True, they are stuffed with all the monsters, trolls, demons and dragons even the most freaky fantasy fan could wish for. There are rites, fights and magic flights; there is gore galore. Muscle-bound warriors grunt and preen; cowards cower; baddies sneer and snarl. But to all this Pratchett adds another, rare and crucial ingredient: seven-times-distilled pure silliness. If Monty Python had invented a role-playing game, the result would be like this.

Pratchett's books are set on Discworld. This is a vast disc supported on the backs of four huge elephants. It is the home of a thousand thousand species of creature, from everyday trolls and elves to mysterious beings of wood, water, air, light, mud – not to mention Mafia heavies, bimbos, winos, film-directors, pyramid-builders and wizards of every degree from Arch-chancellor Wayzygoose to Rincewind (B.mgc, failed). Characters have names like Tomjon, Lio!rt and Gaspode the talking dog; they say things like 'Yarg' (meaning 'Oh no!') and 'OowoowgrhhffrghooOOo' (meaning 'Vy iss it I now am a blue colour?'). A piece of luggage has hundreds of tiny legs and a lid that snaps like shark's teeth.

Pratchett writes one, sometimes one-and-a-half, Discworld books each year. They are self-contained, but characters drop in and out of the series like guests coming and going at some everlasting, lunatic party. Death (who ALWAYS SPEAKS IN CAPITALS), failing to get his man (or rather, wizard) in *The Colour of Magic*, takes an apprentice in *Mort*. Granny Weatherwax the witch features in *Equal Rites* and is given a cackling, Shakespeare-haunted starring role in *Wyrd Sisters* ('When shall we three meet again?' 'Well, I can do next Tuesday'...). Rincewind, the scrawny, cowardly wizard who flunked his magic course and knows only one spell (which he dare not speak) turns up in story after story, like a bad quarter-rhinu from the Counterweight Continent. If anyone so much as thinks the number eight, big trouble follows.

All of this is true, and none of it is to be taken seriously. If you read Pratchett, no other fantasy writer will ever seem the same again.

TRY THESE
**Douglas Adams, *Dirk Gently's Holistic Detective Agency*
Craig Shaw Gardner, *A Malady of Magicks*
Tom Holt, *Expecting Someone Taller***

MR PRATCHETT WOULD LIKE YOU TO MEET:
Binky (horse); Captain Eightpanther (inventor of teeth-shattering Travellers' Digestive Biscuits); Harebut the Provision Merchant (father of Nijel 'the Destroyer'); WxrtHltl-jwlpklz (demon) ... not to mention a talking tree and a trombone-playing cow

See also
Adams, Fantasy and Horror, Tolkien

66 The brown-clad one reached into his tunic and took out a golden disc on a short chain. Bravd raised his eyebrows.
'The wizard said that the little man had some sort of golden disc that told him the time,' said the Weasel.
'Arousing your cupidity, little friend? You always were an expert thief, Weasel.'
'Aye', said the Weasel modestly. He touched the knob at the disc's rim, and it flipped open.
The very small demon imprisoned within looked up from its tiny abacus and scowled. 'It lacks but ten minutes to eight of the clock,' it snarled. The lid snapped shut, almost trapping the Weasel's fingers. 99

MARY RENAULT
THE KING MUST DIE (1958)

● ● ● ● ● ● ● ● ● ● ● ● ● ● ● ●

THE STORY
On Minoan Crete, the bull is god.
The bull-king Minos, in his
labyrinth-palace, demands tribute
from the whole Greek world: young
men and women to dance the
sacred bull-dances and be
sacrificed to the god. Prince
Theseus of Athens takes the place
of one of the young men chosen for
his year. He learns the skills of bull-
leaping, and becomes a court
favourite. He absorbs the manners
and rituals of the effete Cretan
court, without losing sight of his
secret purpose – to topple Minoan
power – or forgetting his personal
loyalty to Poseidon, god of
earthquakes. Eventually, inspired
by the god, he knows that the time
has come to confront the Minotaur
and end Crete's power.

RENAULT, Mary
1905-1983
Real name Mary Challans
South African citizen
Other jobs: nursing
Began writing: 1930s
Other details: born and
educated in Britain.

See also
Dunnett, Graves, Romance of the
Past

━━ ━━ ━━ ━━ ━━ ━━ ━━ ━━

The Greek myths have mesmeric power.
Odysseus, the Wooden Horse, Theseus and
the Minotaur, the Golden Fleece – 3,000
years after they first appeared, such stories
are still among the most haunting, most
often told in the Western world.

Because the myths seem to touch every
aspect of human experience, people down
the centuries have used them as the spring-
board for all kinds of other thought. The
ancient Athenians turned them into tragic
dramas which are still among the peaks of
the art. The emperor Nero is said to have
burned Rome to provide a backdrop while
he recited his own epic poem 'The Sack of
Troy'. The myths have provided (rather less
extreme) inspiration to poets, musicians and
painters from Renaissance times to the present day.

Renault took in all this culture, the
myths and their myriad derivatives, from
childhood on. She responded, as most people do, to the directness and power of the
stories. But she was also interested in the
mindset of the Greeks themselves: the pat-
terns of thought, culture and belief which
led them to create the myths in the first
place, and which the myths helped to pass
on from generation to generation.

In the 1920s, Renault's girlhood, there
was an upsurge of interest in such matters.
It was mainly scholarly, and extremely dry.
But it provided a treasury of information
almost as rich as the myths themselves –
and this interest was reinforced by head-
line-catching archaeological work, for
example Arthur Evans' discovery and con-

troversial restoration of the palace of Knossos in Crete, home of the mythical Minotaur.

In the 1960s, authors who wrote about the past were often influenced by Robert Graves' *I, Claudius*, in which modern psychological attitudes are dazzlingly projected back in time. Renault took a different path entirely. She thought herself back into the skin of her characters, trying to recreate their experience as it might have been, not as if they were ourselves in ancient dress.

The result is a thrilling feeling of authenticity. Renault's research is meticulous, but it never obtrudes (a common failing in books of this kind). She sweeps you along, making you feel that life may very well have been lived like this. And her plots are magnificent, with a sweep and power rivalling those of the myths which inspired her. She had a genius for the past.

OTHER RENAULT NOVELS SET IN GREECE
The Bull from the Sea (sequel)
Fire from Heaven, The Persian Boy, Funeral Games (trilogy about Alexander the Great)
The Last of the Wine
The Mask of Apollo

TRY THESE
Naomi Mitchison, *The Corn King and the Spring Queen*
Henry Treece, *Electra*
Norman Mailer, *Ancient Evenings*
Pär Lagerkvist, *The Sibyl*

66 Horns blew, a door opened behind the shrine. There she stood; I remembered the shape of her, like a field-lily, upright and small, round breasts and thighs, a waist to snap in your fingers. But now she was stiff with gold; you could only see the red of her dress when the flounces stirred. Her foot-high diadem was crested with a golden leopard. If she had not moved, I should have taken her for jeweller's work.

The men all stood, laying fist on breast; the women touched their foreheads. She took her tall throne. There was a music of harps and flutes.

The bull-dancers came in from the door below us. They stepped slowly but lightly, two by two, a girl and a boy, in a solemn dance-step. Their love-locks sleeked and combed bounced on their smooth shoulders, their arm-rings and neck-laces caught the light; the girls' young breasts, and the rumps of their little loin-guards, jigged prettily in the dance ... 99

ROMANCE OF THE PAST

Since tales of Robin Hood were first told, people have enjoyed history with a swagger in its step and colour in its cheeks. In the nineteenth century, Sir Walter Scott (*Ivanhoe*; *Rob Roy*), Victor Hugo (*Les Misérables*; *The Hunchback of Notre Dame*) and Alexandre Dumas (*The Three Musketeers*; *The Count of Monte Cristo*) put this kind of writing on the map, and despite old-fashioned style, their books still stir the blood. Some modern writers have continued the swashbuckling tradition: sea-yarns and army-yarns, for example, are a shelfful in themselves. Other writers explore the romance of the past in more domestic settings, telling tales of the intimate lives of kings and queens, or setting the passions and love-affairs of ordinary people in big houses, towns and villages two or more centuries ago.

BARONESS ORCZY (1865-1947) invented one of the best loved of all adventurers, the Scarlet Pimpernel: by day languid, lisping wimp Sir Percy Blakeney, by night the Scarlet Pimpernel who outsmarts, outduels, outquips the dastardly Chauvelin and his minions, tools of the French Revolution and servants of Madame Guillotine. Recommended title (you guessed): *The Scarlet Pimpernel*.

'JEAN PLAIDY' (Eleanor Hibbert, born 1906) wrote some 80 light novels about the political intrigues and love- affairs of the royal courts of Europe between the twelfth and sixteenth centuries. Recommended titles: *The Bastard King* (first of the 'Norman' Saga, about William the Conqueror); *The Spanish Bridegroom*; *Flaunting Extravagant Queen*. Hibbert also wrote historical romance as 'Philippa Carr' and 'Victoria Holt'.

LLOYD C. DOUGLAS (1877-1951) wrote two powerful novels based on the events of the New Testament, *The Robe* and *The Big Fisherman*. They are not preachy, but colourful and evocative, and superbly show the effects of religious belief on ordinary people's minds.

NORAH LOFTS (1904-1986) wrote romances, mainly set in the eighteenth century. Some are about girls brought up in or coming to live in sinister old houses; others involve the villagers, innkeepers, poachers, smugglers and highwaymen who roamed the East Anglian Fens. Recommended titles: *The House at Old Vine*; *The Brittle Glass*.

MARGARET MITCHELL (1900-1949) wrote *Gone With the Wind*, the historical romance to end them all. It is set in the US Deep South, and the turbulent events leading up to and during the Civil War parallel the stormy passions in Scarlett O'Hara's breast as she is torn between two men, foppish Ashley Wilkes and cynical, rakish Rhett Butler. Alexandra Ripley's *Scarlett* is an authorized sequel, published 60 years after the original book.

STEPHEN MARLOWE (born 1928) has written books of every kind from space opera to fairy tale. He is nowadays best known for blockbuster fictionalized 'autobiographies'. Recommended titles: *The Memoirs of Christopher Columbus*; *The Death and Life of Miguel Cervantes*.

C.S. FORESTER (1899-1966) invented Horatio Hornblower, a career navy officer at the time of Nelson. Recommended title: *The Happy Return* (first in the series). Hornblower inspired equally lively series by other writers, including Dudley Pope and Alexander Kent (sea stories) and Bernard Cornwell and George McDonald Frazer (army stories).

See also

Brontë, Du Maurier, Heyer, Hope, Stevenson

TRY THESE

Frans Bengtsson, *The Long Ships*

Jean M. Auel, *The Plains of Passage*

James Clavell, *Shôgun*

Rosalind Laker, *What the Heart Keeps*

T.N. Murari, *Taj*

Edward Rutherfurd, *Sarum*

E.V. Thompson, *The Restless Sea*

Frank Yerby, *The Foxes of Harrow*

From *Tilly Trotter* by 'Catherine Cookson' (Anne McMullen, born 1906):

66 The housekeeper was now joined by the butler. Mr Pike was a man nearing seventy. He had a long, tired face, his shoulders were slightly stooped, and when he looked at her his eyes gave nothing away – his gaze was neutral.

'Well, let's get it over. Come, girl,' said the housekeeper.

'Does she want to see her tonight?'

The housekeeper turned her head to look at the butler.

'My order from Her Ladyship Price was to take her up as soon as she arrived.'

'What has the mistress got to do with it when that one's about? Come on, you.' 99

(Other Cookson novels: *Tilly Trotter Wed*; *Tilly Trotter Widowed*; The 'Mallen' trilogy, beginning with *The Mallen Girl*; the 'Mary Ann' books, beginning with *A Grand Man*)

SCIENCE FICTION AND FANTASY

Science fiction was invented at the end of the nineteenth century, by such writers as Jules Verne and H. G. Wells. In the early days, writers were chiefly interested in the 'science' side of it. Books were crammed with details of the new inventions and applications of scientific processes, mostly concerned with exploration of outer and inner space. Writers of the time assumed that the human race would colonize alien planets and their inhabitants by right, that Earth would rule OK. But as science fiction grew more sophisticated, writers began using it to air all kinds of moral, ethical, political, religious and social questions – the *why* of what people did became as important as the *how*. There was, and is, a strong feeling that writing about imaginary worlds allows us to explore the entire situation of humanity. In modern science fiction, there are also strong elements of satire and surrealism.

ISAAC ASIMOV (1920-1992) was hugely prolific, and wrote non-fiction as well as fiction, the latter good on scientific and technological theory (he was particularly interested in robotics) and on 'problem solving', but it also deals with the sociological and ethical problems of his invented worlds. Recommended start-point: *Foundation* (first of the 'Foundation' series).

URSULA K. LEGUIN (born 1929) writes of a far-distant future, in which a galaxy-wide society believes in such religious and ethical ideas as universal harmony, the importance of symmetry and balance. Romantic, poetic style. Recommended start-point: *The Left Hand of Darkness.*

GENE WOLFE (born 1931) writes what at first appears to be a fantasy rather than science fiction; explorations of unknown worlds. But each world is only the framework for Wolfe's description of his hero's self-discovery, of his progress through all states of human experience and behaviour towards becoming a united, single personality, our race transfigured in a single being. Recommended start-point: *The Shadow of the Torturer* (first in the four-book series 'The Book of the New Sun').

FRANK HERBERT (1920-1986) was interested in the nature of intelligence – whether human intelligence is the only kind possible, and what the consequences might be if we could tinker with our minds. Best known for his sequence of 'Dune' books, in which all human history is re-enacted, as it were, but differently, on an alien, desert world.

WALTER M. MILLER (born 1922) wrote one of the great classics of science fiction, the post-apocalypse fantasy *A Canticle for Leibowitz*, about how the human race, after nuclear devastation, has to reinvent its scientific and ethical culture, avoiding (if possible) the mistakes it made first time round.

PHILIP K. DICK (1928-1982) wrote about alternative reality, delving into the fantasies of deranged or drug-inspired minds – the 'alien' environments lurking inside our own heads. Recommended start-point: *The Man in the High Castle* (in which Germany and Japan have won the Second World War – if this is truly the 'real' world we think it is).

MICHAEL MOORCOCK (born 1939) wrote the Jerry Cornelius books: dreamlike fantasies set in an alternative world in which time is a mist rather than a sequence, surreality rules and imagination outranks fact. Recommended start-point: *The Final Programme*.

TRY THESE

Brian W. Aldiss, *Helliconia Spring*

James Blish, *A Case of Conscience*

Philip José Farmer, *To Your Scattered Bodies Go*

Harry Harrison, *Make Room! Make Room!*

Robert Heinlein, *Stranger in a Strange Land*

Larry Niven, *Protector*

Frederick Pohl, *Gateway*

EARLY SCIENCE FICTION

Jules Verne, *Journey to the Centre of the Earth*

H. G. Wells, *The Time Machine*

C. S. Lewis, *Out of the Silent Planet*

John Wyndham, *The Day of the Triffids*

SATIRE AND COMEDY

Douglas Adams, *Dirk Gently's Holistic Detective Agency*

Harry Harrison, *The Technicolor Time Machine*

Frederick Pohl and C. M. Kornbluth, *The Space Merchants*

Robert Sheckley, *Journey Beyond Tomorrow*

Kurt Vonnegut, *The Sirens of Titan*

See also

Adams, Pratchett, Vonnegut

● ● ● ● ● ● ● ● ● ● ● ● ● ● ● ● ● ●

" From *Rendezvous with Rama* by Arthur C. Clarke (born 1917): And now he understood the purpose of those mysterious trenches, the Straight Valley and its five companions: they were nothing less than gigantic striplights. Rama had six linear suns, symmetrically arranged around its interior. From each, a broad fan of light was aimed across the central axis, to shine upon the far side of the world. Norton wondered if they could be switched alternately to produce a cycle of light and dark-ness, or whether this was a planet of perpetual day.

Too much staring at those blinding bars of light had made his eyes hurt again; he was not sorry to have a good excuse to close them for a while. It was not until then, when he had almost recovered from this initial visual shock, that he was able to devote himself to a much more serious problem. "

(Other Clarke novels: *A Fall of Moondust*; *Imperial Earth*; *The City and the Stars*; *2001*)

SHORT STORIES

● ●

The best short stories take single events or aspects of experience, and distil them in a handful of pages. They are often written at a single sitting, in a single flush of inspiration rather than the slow gestation of a novel – and this gives them packed power. A few writers conceive their collections as units, intending the stories to be read together. But most stories are written for single publication in magazines, and reading them one after another, in book form, can lessen their effect. Browsing and sampling restores individuality, makes each story stand out from its surroundings rather than seeming like just one more brick in a solid wall.

ERNEST HEMINGWAY (1898-1961) wrote 'he-man' stories about hunting, shooting, fishing, boxing and brawling. But they are not all they seem: Hemingway concentrates on his heroes' feet of clay, the fragile humanity under the cocky façade. Good collections: *Men Without Women*, *Winner Take Nothing*.

JOHN CHEEVER (1912-1982) wrote of middle-class Americans (like the families in yuppie soaps and sitcoms), showing the bleak side of their adulteries, self-doubts, inadequacies and failures. Good collections: *The Enormous Radio*; *The Brigadier and the Golf Widow*.

V.S. PRITCHETT (born 1900) wrote of seedy-genteel, lower-middle-class life in 1920s–1960s Britain. His stories are like sad, hilarious snapshots of people you never want to meet. Good collections: *The Camberwell Beauty*; *When My Girl Comes Home*.

'SAKI' (H.H. Munro, 1870-1916) wrote satirical, macabre stories about ordinary people who take on something simple (adultery, say, or buying a ferret), and find it escalating out of control in a satanic, bitter world in which human beings are not controllers but victims. Savage fun. Good collections: *The Chronicles of Clovis*; *Beasts and Super-Beasts*.

I.B. SINGER (1904-1991) wrote of two kinds of people: orthodox Jews living in Polish ghetto-villages in the nineteenth century and modern Jewish Americans, haunted by the Holocaust. Ghosts, devils and angels play featured parts. Good collections: *A Friend of Kafka*; *A Crown of Feathers*; *The Spinoza of Market Street*.

FRANZ KAFKA (1883-1924) wrote of grotesque, baffling happenings as if they were everyday reality. A man turns into a giant cockroach. A creature describes its brilliant underground system of tunnels - which engulfs it. A concentration-camp commandant invents a punishment-machine which harrows human flesh. Good collection: *Metamorphosis and Other Stories*.

TRY THESE

Collections: Maeve Binchy, *The Lilac Bus*; Italo Calvino, *Cosmicomics*; Anton Chekhov, *The Lady With the Little Dog*; Jane Gardam, *Flying the Flag*; Susan Hill, *A Bit of Singing and Dancing*; W. Somerset Maugham, *Complete Short Stories*; J.D. Salinger, *Franny and Zooey*; John Updike, *Pigeon Feathers*; Angus Wilson, *A Bit Off the Map*

From 'The Daughters of the Late Colonel' (from collection *The Garden Party*, 1922) by Katherine Mansfield (1888-1923):

" Another thing which complicated matters was they had Nurse Andrews staying on with them that week. It was their own fault; they had asked her. It was Josephine's idea. On the morning – well, on the last morning, when the doctor had gone, Josephine had said to Constantia, 'Don't you think it would be rather nice if we asked Nurse Andrews to stay on for a week as our guest?'

'Very nice,' said Constantia.

'I thought,' went on Josephine quickly, 'I should just say this afternoon, after I've paid her, "My sister and I would be very pleased, after all you've done for us, Nurse Andrews, if you would stay on for a week as our guest." I'd have to put that in about being our guest in case –'

'Oh, but she could hardly expect to be paid!' cried Constantia.

'One never knows,' said Josephine sagely.

Nurse Andrews had, of course, jumped at the idea. But it was a bother. It meant they had to have regular sit-down meals at the proper times, whereas if they'd been alone they could just have asked Kate if she wouldn't mind bringing them a tray wherever they were. And meal-times now that the strain was over were rather a trial.

Nurse Andrews was simply fearful about butter ... "

(Other Mansfield collections: *Bliss*; *The Dove's Nest*; *Something Childish*)

GEORGES SIMENON
THE PATIENCE OF MAIGRET (1965)

● ● ● ● ● ● ● ● ● ● ● ● ● ● ● ● ●

THE STORY

For years Maigret has been trying to link the gangster Manuel Palmari with a series of jewel thefts. The trail seems to have gone cold, when another theft occurs. Maigret visits Palmari, who claims to have retired – and a few hours later, Palmari is mysteriously shot dead. Maigret settles to observe the people and atmosphere of the apartment block in which Palmari lived with his pretty young wife. He is sure that the murderer lives in one of the block's fourteen flats, and that it is simply a matter of placidly watching and waiting, till the truth comes out.

SIMENON, Georges
1903-1989
Belgian citizen
First jobs: seaman; journalist
Began writing: 1920s
Other details: claimed in his autobiography to have had sex with 10,000 different women.

TRY THESE

Nicolas Freeling, *Dressing of Diamond* (Amsterdam)
James Melville, *The Wages of Zen* (Tokyo)
Magdalen Nabb, *Death of a Dutchman* (Florence)

Simenon wrote more than 500 novels, sometimes as many as ten a year. Most are tense psychological thrillers. But outside French-speaking countries, he is best known for a long series of novels (over 80) starring Chief Inspector Maigret of the Paris Police Judiciaire.

Maigret is middle-aged, large and comfortable. He and his wife live unremarkable, even boring lives. If you passed them in the street, you would hardly notice them.

Lack of noticeability is Maigret's main professional asset. His 'method' is to have no method at all. Often, when he takes on a case, he avoids reading the details till later. Instead, he goes to the location of the crime, and sets about soaking up its atmosphere. He sits in cafés and bars, unobtrusive as an old dog in a corner, until he knows the people and their surroundings as well as if he'd lived there all his life.

Simenon's accounts of this stage of investigation, soaking up the atmosphere, are wonderfully evocative. Most Maigret books are set in Paris, and as Maigret sits and savours, so do we. Simenon's Paris is all you would expect from 1950s travel posters – tree-lined boulevards, Montmartre, the Métro, croissants, Gauloises – but it also has the texture of a real, live place. The look of the stones, the babble of passing crowds, the feel of rain or sun – Simenon builds his picture from a hundred such details, in an unhurried way exactly in tune with Maigret's character.

About halfway through each book, Maigret makes his move. He isolates one suspect, either at the person's home or in his own pipe-smoke-filled office at Police Headquarters, and begins to talk. In the hands of most other detectives, this talking would be an interrogation. With Maigret it seems more like leisurely conversation – except that it returns, question after gentle question, to the person's home life, family, feelings and actions on the crucial day.

Maigret has often been filmed, and has been twice televised in English. But because the stories depend so much on atmosphere and lack of action, they are hard to realize on screen. In book-form, as conceived, they are magnificent.

NON-MAIGRET SIMENON NOVELS
The Man Who Watched the Trains Go By
Blind Alley
Act of Passion
The Watchmaker
Inquest on Bouvet

OTHER 'MAIGRET' NOVELS
Maigret and the Burglar's Wife
My Friend Maigret
Madame Maigret's Friend
Maigret Sets a Trap

See also
Crime and Thrillers, Dexter, Paretsky

66 When Maigret left home that morning, he'd no idea that he'd end up in the Rue des Acacias, where he'd spent so many frustrating hours the week before. It was a sunny morning, and a pleasure he shared with millions of other Parisians. He'd no idea, either, that at about one o'clock he'd be lunching with Magistrate Ancelin in the bistro Chez l'Auvergnat.

The bistro was opposite Palmari's: a bar like they used to be, with a zinc counter, aperitifs which only a few old customers still drank, the patron in his blue apron, sleeves rolled up, face slashed by a glossy black moustache.

Hanging from the ceiling, sausages of every kind; gourd-shaped cheeses; grey-skinned hams that looked as if they'd been smoked in ash; on a shelf, flat wheels of bread all the way from the Massif Central. In the kitchen, just visible through the hatch of the door, the owner's thin, dried-up wife, busy at her stove.

'Table for two? For lunch?'

On the oil-cloth table-top, instead of a table-cloth, a sheet of sugar-paper. The patron would use it to work out the bill. Chalked on a panel on the wall, the menu ... 99

R. L . STEVENSON
KIDNAPPED (1886)

● ● ● ● ● ● ● ● ● ● ● ● ● ● ● ●

THE STORY

David Balfour, an orphan, leaves
the village where he was brought up
and goes to seek his fortune. He
makes his way to the house of an
uncle he has never met – and who
shows great fear of him and goes to
great lengths to dispose of him.
David is kidnapped by an evil sea-
captain to be sold as a slave. But he
is rescued by Alan Breck, who
embroils him in the attempt to bring
James Stuart to power. There is a
murder; David and Breck are hunted
across the Highlands by the English
and Scots loyal to the English
crown. It takes most of the book for
David to come through this
adventure – and he still has his
uncle to face and a score to settle.

> STEVENSON, Robert Louis
> 1850-1894
> British citizen
> First jobs: trainee advocate;
> journalist
> Began to write: 1870s
> Other details: travelled
> widely (writing still enjoyable
> books about France,
> California and the South
> Seas); spent his last years on
> Samoa.

TRY THESE

Walter Scott, *Rob Roy*
Jeffrey Farnol, *The Broad Highway*
John Buchan, *The Thirty-Nine Steps*
    (modern)
Geoffrey Household, *Rogue Male*
    (modern)

The first thing you notice about
Kidnapped is its language. It is perfectly
easy to understand, but instead of the
'standard English' usual in novels, it is
Highland Scots, as individual and particular as modern Indian or Caribbean English.
The words Stevenson uses are standard,
give or take a few dialect expressions
(translated in footnotes). But they flow
with a music of their own, a seductive,
almost poetic ebb and flow. The story
itself is breathless high adventure: thirty
short chapters, each bustling with action,
sharp dialogue, twists and surprises. The
villains, and their plans for the hero
(embezzlement, kidnap, slavery, murder),
are as black-hearted as anyone could wish.
But the obvious never happens quite as
you expect: Stevenson's story-teller's cunning makes even the corniest plot ideas
seem astonishing and new.

Kidnapped tells David Balfour's adventures in the eighteenth year of his life.
It sends him on a journey round the coasts
and across the mountains and glens of
Scotland, and matches that with an emotional journey from boy to man. At the
book's heart is David's relationship with
Alan Breck, the mysterious, reckless
stranger who becomes his friend and protector, and who leads him into the morass
of Jacobite politics (Breck supports the
claims of James Stuart to the throne of
Scotland), into murder, manhunt and all-
but civil war. Breck's character is fascinating, and Stevenson reveals it gradually,
always showing it through David's eyes.

And in the same way as David learns manhood, so to speak, by observing Breck, so he also discovers his own country, crisscrossing it to evade pursuit and observing the full range of its people and their attitudes to religion, politics and the other affairs of life. Stevenson works the same magic with content as he does with style. The book does the work. It presents a world which is complete, attractive and accessible; all we have to do is read.

OTHER STEVENSON NOVELS
Catriona (sequel)
The Master of Ballantrae
The Black Arrow
The Strange Case of Dr Jekyll and Mr Hyde
Treasure Island (not entirely the children's book films and TV suggest)

See also
Doyle, Hope

66 The soldiers began to spread, some of them to run, and others to put up their pieces and cover me; and still I stood.
'Jouk in here among the trees,' said a voice, close by. Indeed, I scarce knew what I was doing, but I obeyed, and as I did so, I heard the firelocks bang and the balls whistle in the birches.

Just inside the shelter of the trees I found Alan Breck standing, with a fishing-rod. He gave me no salutation; indeed it was no time for civilities; only 'Come!' says he, and set off running along the side of the mountain towards Balachulish; and I, like a sheep, to follow him.

Now we ran among the birches; now stooping behind low humps upon the mountain side; now crawling on all fours among the heather. The pace was deadly; my heart seemed bursting against my ribs; and I had neither time to think nor breath to speak with. Only I remember seeing with wonder, that Alan every now and then would straighten himself to his full height and look back; and every time he did so, there came a great far-away cheering and crying of the soldiers ... 99

IRVING STONE
THE AGONY AND THE ECSTASY (1961)

●●●●●●●●●●●●●●●●●

THE STORY

This book covers Michelangelo's life from his thirteenth birthday, when he apprenticed himself to the great Florentine painter Ghirlandaio, to his lonely, wracked death some 78 years later. He worked for – and quarrelled with – the Medici in Florence and the Pope in Rome. He designed the St Peter's we know today. He created a handful of the world's most treasured artistic masterpieces. And, as Stone tells it, he was a man of turbulent, volcanic passion, constantly being brought back from the abyss of rage or carnal obsession by his devotion to God and to the imperious demands of his genius and his craft.

STONE, Irving
1903-1989
US citizen
Other jobs: art critic, teacher of biographical writing
Began writing: 1930s
Other details: also wrote non-fiction about figures in US life: *Clarence Darrow for the Defence*; *Earl Warren*; *They Also Ran – the Story of the Men who were Defeated for the Presidency*.

For most of this century, a favourite form of Hollywood entertainment has been the biopic. In this, basically, a star plays a star. In a kind of double exposure, we see both Moses and Charlton Heston, both Barbra Streisand and Fanny Brice, both Abraham Lincoln and Henry Fonda, both Roger Daltrey and Franz Liszt. Star actors help us identify with the flesh-and-bloodness of famous people of the past, even if the scriptwriters' notion of how such people talk is occasionally off the mark: 'Hi, Mozart. Have you met Beethoven? You'll have to speak up, he's a little deaf.'

Without ever reaching such heights of silliness, Stone produced a dozen 'biopic' novels, best-sellers about such people as Abraham Lincoln's wife, Van Gogh, the US politician Eugene V. Debs, Charles Darwin. Each is based on a mountain of research. Stone describes the clothes, food, houses, ways of speech, attitudes and way of life of the period in stitch-by-stitch detail, and the effect is as vivid as if black-and-white photos or engravings had blossomed into technicolor and begun to move.

In a biographical novel, of course, we are denied the presence of a great film star. Stone gets round this by giving star-prominence to the actual work his people do. Few writers are so good at making us feel what it must be like to conduct a political meeting in the White House, to plead a case in court, to go through the processes of scientific observation and deduction which led to the Theory of Evolution, or to paint the Sistine Chapel ceiling.

Michelangelo is an ideal subject for such a writer. His life spanned the greatest years of the Italian Renaissance – indeed, in Rome and in Florence, he gave that Renaissance the definitive look it still has in our mind's eye, and in reality, today. He wrote obsessively about himself in letters, diaries and poems. Nothing is 'secret' about him or his work, except the central mystery of what it was like to have such a talent and how it functioned. Stone is no more able to explain that than anyone else, even Michelangelo himself. But if you want a day-by-day picture of Renaissance Italian life, and a chip-by-chip, drip-by-drip account of how one chisels statues from marble or covers acres of ceiling with Bible scenes which express the heart of one's own religious belief, this book is unbeatable.

OTHER STONE NOVELS
Lust for Life (Van Gogh)
The Passions of the Mind (Freud)
The Origin (Darwin)
Love is Eternal (Mary Todd Lincoln)

TRY THESE
Stephen Marlowe, *The Memoirs of Christopher Columbus*
Joseph Skvorecky, *Dvorak in Love*
Alan Brien, *Lenin, the Novel*
William Golding, *The Spire*

See also
Dunnett, Graves

66 'There's a scaffolding that will hold you securely for the rest of your life.'
  'You'd like to think so, Bramante, but actually it will only be a matter of months.' Bramante stuck in his throat like a half-swallowed fly. The Pope by himself would hardly have thought of inflicting this ceiling on him. He inspected the scaffolding, knit his brows. 'Just what do you intend to do with the holes in the ceiling after the poles come out?'
  'Fill them.'
  'How do we get up to the holes to fill them after the scaffolding is down? Ride on an eagle's back?'
  '... I hadn't thought of that.'
  'Nor of what we are to do with forty ugly cement fills in the middle of my painting after I have finished the job. Let's discuss it with the pontiff.' 99

J. R. R. TOLKIEN
THE LORD OF THE RINGS (1954-5)

●●●●●●●●●●●●●●●●●

THE STORY

Gandalf the wizard persuades a hobbit, Frodo, to try to save the world by taking the Ring of Power back to its place of origin, the Cracks of Doom, and destroying it. This will prevent Sauron and his dark forces from overwhelming all creation. Frodo, his faithful servant Sam and a band of companions set out to find the Cracks of Doom. On the way they face perils and adversaries of all kinds, from Sauron's demon-riders to the corrupt and devious Gollum. They are, however, helped by beings of good, as the whole world takes sides for a final, climactic battle between Light and Dark.

> TOLKIEN, John Ronald Ruell
> 1892-1973
> British citizen
> Day job: professor at Oxford
> University
> Began writing: 1910s
> Other details: works became
> a hippy cult in the 1960s,
> the days of Flower Power;
> Tolkien (then over 70)
> complained that he didn't
> know how to cope with fan
> letters starting 'Hey, man'
> and ending 'Peace'.

See also
Fantasy and Horror, Pratchett

Tolkien began by creating a language (Elvish). Then he invented a people to talk it, and a world for them to live in. He made up myths and legends about this world, and told them to his children as bedtime stories. Out of this grew his first book, *The Hobbit* – and seventeen years later its sequel, the *Lord of the Rings* trilogy.

By the time Tolkien wrote *The Hobbit*, his imaginary world was crammed, not just with elves, but with creatures of every kind from dwarfs to wizards, from dragons and orcs to the friendly, lazy hobbits which were his own favourite creation.

The Hobbit was a straightforward tale about an unwilling hero persuaded to join a group of quarrelsome dwarfs on a quest to steal a dragon's hoard. *The Lord of the Rings* is more complex, adding adult themes to basic adventure. The quest this time is nothing less than a mission to save the world. The forces of light (hobbits, elves, wizards, dwarfs and others) are ranged against the forces of darkness (led by the evil wizard Sauron), and many other beings, including humans, are caught in the middle.

In such a saga, magic and chance are still important. But events are chiefly controlled by the play between the different characters' personalities and moralities. Moral strength is a source of power; it waxes and wanes according to the choices characters make at each crisis-point.

This moral wavering gives the story density and power. Another main attraction is Tolkien's amazing, dotty imagination. He took ideas from everywhere – Egyptian myth, Norse sagas, the Arabian Nights, Walt Disney's Snow White. He stuffed the book with snippets of the myths, history and songs of his imaginary world, and at the back of the last volume he outlined that history and those languages, in such detail that members of the Tolkien Society can still write myth-poetry and talk to each other in Entish, Elvish or Orc.

Tolkien invented the fantasy novel, and thousands of other writers have followed him. But few can equal the sheer, satisfying completeness of his world. Detail was his obsession, and it is the glory of his book.

OTHER TOLKIEN BOOKS

The Silmarillion (myths and legends from the early history of Tolkien's imaginary country, hundreds of generations before the events of *The Hobbit* or *The Lord of the Rings*)

There are several books of short tales, edited and published after Tolkien's death. They should fascinate addicts, but may bore others. Good collections: *Unfinished Tales*; *The Book of Lost Tales*.

TRY THESE

Stephen Donaldson, *The Chronicles of Thomas Covenant*

David Eddings, *The Mallorean*

Clive Barker, *Weaveworld*

C.S. Lewis, *Voyage to Venus/Perelandra* (science fiction good-versus-evil story by a friend of Tolkien)

66 'Let go, Gollum,' he said. 'This is Sting. You have seen it before once upon a time. Let go, or you'll feel it this time! I'll cut your throat.'

Gollum collapsed and went as loose as wet string. Sam got up, fingering his shoulder. His eyes smouldered with anger, but he could not avenge himself: his miserable enemy lay grovelling on the stones whimpering.

'Don't hurt us! Don't let them hurt us, precious! They won't hurt us will they, nice little hobbitses? We didn't mean no harm, but they jumps on us like cats on poor mices, they did, precious. And we're so lonely, gollum. We'll be nice to them, very nice, if they'll be nice to us, won't we, yes, yess.' 99

ANTHONY TROLLOPE

BARCHESTER TOWERS (1857)

● ● ● ● ● ● ● ● ● ● ● ● ● ● ● ●

THE STORY

Barchester Towers is a comedy about domestic and cathedral politics. Mrs Proudie, imperious wife of the timid new Bishop of Barchester, brings the Reverend Obadiah Slope into the Palace to help her dominate her husband and run the diocese. But although Slope seems deferential to the point of sliminess, he is actually interested only in his own advancement, and plots and schemes behind Mrs Proudie's back. Their silky power-struggle gradually engulfs everyone else in the story: mousy Bishop Proudie, charming Mrs Bold, flirtatious Signora Vesey-Neroni, stormy Archdeacon Grantly, pathetic but prolific Parson Quiverful and his fourteen squalling brats.

> ○ TROLLOPE, Anthony
> ○ 1815-82
> ○ British citizen
> ○ Day job: Post Office official
> ○ Began writing: 1840s
> ○ Other details: still renowned
> ○ in Post Office circles
> ○ for introducing the pillar box
> ○ to Britain.

THE 'BARSETSHIRE CHRONICLES' IN ORDER

The Warden; Barchester Towers; Doctor Thorne; Framley Parsonage; The Small House at Allington; The Last Chronicle of Barset

━ ━ ━ ━ ━ ━ ━ ━ ━ ━

Trollope prided himself on being a shining example of Victorian hard work and enterprise. He held a full-time job involving a huge amount of travelling. Even so, from his late twenties onwards, he trained himself to get up at 5.30 every day except Sunday, wherever he was, and write for three hours, producing exactly three thousand words. Working this way, he completed 47 novels, a dozen non-fiction books, dozens of short stories, and the *Autobiography* from which these facts are taken.

Trollope's painstaking approach affected the style of his books as well as their production. He avoided suggestion and allusion; everything had to be made explicit. Whatever he was writing about, he described in scrupulous detail: the weather, the way people dressed and ate, their work, their thoughts and their emotions. In true Victorian style, his books are pictures of their time; but they are mosaics, thousands of tiny pieces exactly placed, rather than the swaggering panoramas of other writers of his time.

Trollope's best-known books are two six-novel sequences, the 'Barsetshire Chronicles' and the 'Palliser' novels. Each book is self-contained, but the same characters reappear, and the background and general areas of concern are similar throughout each sequence. The Barsetshire books centre on the middle class of a small county town, with cathedral gossip and intrigue leading in some books to tragedy, in others to comedy. The 'Palliser' novels deal with local and national politics, and are mainly straight-faced, though Trollope's ridicule of Westminster and High Court pomposity leads to scenes of spectacular farce.

Trollope was by no means the grey 'chronicler of the ordinary' his civil-service working methods might suggest. He had a deadpan sense of humour, and was merciless (in a polite, mid-nineteenth-century way, but none the less lethal for all that) to humbug, vanity and silliness. Given the sort of people he wrote about – Victorian worthies and their feather-brained spouses – he had plenty of targets for mockery, and hit every one bull's-eye.

THE 'PALLISER' NOVELS IN ORDER
Can You Forgive Her?; *Phineas Finn*; *The Eustace Diamond*; *Phineas Redux*; *The Prime Minister*; *The Duke's Children*

TRY THESE
Angela Thirkell, *High Rising* (first of a sequence set in Barsetshire)
Benjamin Disraeli, *Coningsby* (good follow-up to the 'Palliser' books)
Mrs Gaskell, *Cranford*
John Galsworthy, *The Man of Property*
C.P. Snow, *The Master*

See also
Austen, Dickens, Fowles, Heyer

❝ 'Bishop,' said the lady, as his lordship sat himself down, 'don't sit on that sofa, if you please; it is to be kept separate for a lady.'

The bishop jumped up and seated himself on a cane-bottomed chair. 'A lady?' he inquired meekly; 'do you mean one particular lady, my dear?'

'Yes, Bishop, one particular lady,' said his wife, disdaining to explain.

'She has got no legs, papa,' said the youngest daughter, tittering.

'No legs!' said the bishop, opening his eyes.

'Nonsense, Netta, what stuff you talk,' said Olivia. 'She has got legs, but she can't use them. She has always to be kept lying down, and three or four men carry her about everywhere.'

'Laws, how odd!' said Augusta. 'Always carried about by four men! I'm sure I shouldn't like it. Am I right behind, Mamma? I feel as if I was open'; and she turned her back to her anxious parent.

'Open! To be sure you are,' said she ... and Mrs Proudie poked the strings here, and twitched the dress there, and gave her daughter a shove and a shake, and then pronounced it all right. ❞

MARK TWAIN
HUCKLEBERRY FINN (1884)

● ● ● ● ● ● ● ● ● ● ● ● ● ● ● ●

THE STORY

Huck has been given half the reward for capturing Injun Joe (in *Tom Sawyer*), and his wastrel father wants the money and kidnaps him. Huck escapes down-river on a raft with Jim, a runaway slave. At every turn they are beset by conmen, bounty-hunters and outraged citizens, and they fall into slapstick adventures each time they land. But for all the fun and games, they are still inescapably on the run, and the question of their future – will Jim be sent back to slavery, Huck be adopted by some well-meaning widow? – gives underlying tension to every page of the story, till Huck finally resolves it and ends the book.

> TWAIN, Mark
> 1835-1910
> **Real name Samuel Langhorn Clemens**
> US citizen
> First jobs: printer's apprentice (from age twelve); silver-prospector; journalist
> Began writing: journalism 1850s; fiction 1860s
> Other details: fought for two weeks in the Civil War, before being invalided out; Halley's Comet appeared on the day he was born, and he later swore that he would die on the day it reappeared. He did.

Huckleberry Finn is a sequel to Twain's earlier novel *Tom Sawyer* – in the sense that it uses many of the same characters, and carries the story on from where *Tom Sawyer* left off. But its density and seriousness lift it to a completely different plane, so much so that the two books could almost be by different authors.

Tom Sawyer is a children's book. It tells the adventures of two boys growing up on the banks of the Mississippi in the innocent years before the American Civil War. Innocence is the key-word. The boys are at that late pre-pubertal stage when they are old enough to judge adult behaviour, but have no real sense of the underlying issues and resonance of life. They carry no moral burdens: life may have moments of threat or darkness, but essentially it is like a game. Adults in *Tom Sawyer* are stereotypes, stern, kind, silly or threatening; good and evil are straight-cut issues; there are neither doubts nor compromise.

In *Huckleberry Finn*, Tom Sawyer still sees everything in these Garden-of-Eden terms. But for Huck, a few months older, everything has changed. He still behaves as cheerily, recklessly, cockily as ever, but now he notices that issues can be complex, that there are shades of interpretation, that cause and effect play their part in life. Since he narrates the story, we share his viewpoint – something which allows Twain to recap all the kinds of people and behaviour from the earlier book, showing us facets he ignored before.

Twain's blend of wit and fury is similar to Dickens', and he also rivals Dickens as a creator of larger-than-life characters and a tortuous, ever-engrossing plot. But he is much tougher-minded: witty where Dickens is sentimental, preferring realism or irony to the melodrama of Dickens. *Huckleberry Finn* is a warmly credible picture of a boy growing up – and a sprawling panorama of mid-nineteenth-century Southern US life. The book is exciting and comic, but it also makes political and social points which are still stingingly relevant, and very dark indeed.

66 So she put me up a snack, and says: 'Say – when a cow's laying down, which end of her gets up first? Answer up prompt, now – don't stop to study over it. Which end gets up first?'
'The hind end, mum.'
'Well, then, a horse?'
'The for'ard end, mum.'
'Which side of a tree does the most moss grow on?'
'North side.'
'If fifteen cows is browsing on a hillside, how many of them eats with their heads pointing in the same direction?'
'The whole fifteen, mum.'
'Well, I reckon you have lived in the country. I thought maybe you was trying to hocus me again. What's your real name, now?'
'George Peters, mum.'
'Well, try to remember it, George. Don't forget and tell me it's Elexander before you do, and then get out by saying it's George-Elexander when I catch you ...' 99

ANNE TYLER
MORGAN'S PASSING (1980)

●●●●●●●●●●●●●●●

THE STORY

Morgan has been married for nineteen years, and lives in easy-going harmony with his wife, mother, sister and seven teenage daughters. He also inhabits a dream-world of his own, imagining himself a postman, Russian immigrant, detective, as the mood of the moment takes him. One day he meets Leon and Emily Meredith – and becomes obsessed: first by how different their lives are from his, then by them personally, and eventually by Emily in particular. As the book proceeds, we are encouraged to wonder whether Morgan's obsession and its effects on him and all the other characters are destroying what was true and real before, or are like a door, opening into true reality, true happiness, for everyone involved.

● TYLER, Anne Modaressi
● Born 1941
● US citizen
● First job: Russian-language
● bibliographer at Columbia
● University
● Began writing: 1960s
● Other details: writes for *New
● Yorker* magazine.

MORE TYLER BOOKS
The Accidental Tourist
The Tin Can Tree
Breathing Lessons
Searching for Caleb
Saint Maybe

In Western countries generally, and the US in particular, there is a cosy myth about family life. It is common in advertisements, TV sitcoms, and films such as *Back to the Future* or *E.T.*.

In this myth, all families are a convenient size: two parents, one-to-three children well-spaced in age. They live in large, warm houses, filled with the friendly clutter of family life: well-worn furniture, sports equipment, dog-baskets, dirty clothes. They squabble wittily and amiably, but hug and bond at the slightest threat from the outside world. Their family unit is a safe haven; storms happen outside it, somewhere else.

Tyler's novels take this myth, and put bombs under it. As each book begins, something happens, or one character reaches a point of emotional no-return, and nothing is the same again. Someone dies; a child is hurt in a road accident; a wife decides to leave her husband; a new acquaintance (not yet a friend or lover) is made.

Tyler describes this process of emotional evolution in functional, calm prose. She is like a quiet-voiced relative telling you a piece of family news – and the effect, when the voice doesn't change but the news becomes ever more scandalous, is compulsive. If you once get into a Tyler story – and some start slowly – you may find it hard to put down.

TV and films may seem, at first sight, to have made this pebble-rippling-the-pool material too familiar. But when you watch the films and sitcoms mentioned above, not to mention such things as *thirtysomething*, *On Golden Pond*, even *Ghost* or *Dynasty*, you are like an eavesdropper, interested only in the particular story and people set in front of you. Tyler's use of the novel-form, and the skill of her writing, offer extra subtlety, deeper satisfaction. You are certainly eavesdropping on one specific family's problems, but Tyler – insidiously, without a word said – is also giving you hints about yourself, about the emotional dilemmas of the human race at large.

> His daughters ate in a separate flurry of gossip and quarrels and giggles – seven slim, blue-jeaned girls and then someone else, a little white-haired waif with rhinestone ear studs, some friend of Kate's. She sat between Kate and Amy and stared at Morgan narrowly, as if she disapproved of him. It made him nervous. He was never truly happy if he felt that even the most random passing stranger found him unlikeable. He'd begun the meal in a fine mood, twirling his spaghetti theatrically on his fork and speaking in a broad Italian accent, but gradually he lost his enthusiasm. 'What d'you keep looking at?' he asked now. 'Have we met before?'
>
> 'Sir?'
>
> 'This is Coquette,' Kate told him.
>
> 'Ah. Coquette.'
>
> 'Me and her are in the same class at school. We like the same boy.'
>
> Morgan frowned. 'Same what?' he said.
>
> 'This boy named Jackson Epps.'
>
> 'But you're only in fifth grade!'
>
> 'We liked him in fourth grade too.'

JOHN UPDIKE
THE CENTAUR (1963)

● ● ● ● ● ● ● ● ● ● ● ● ● ● ● ● ●

THE STORY

During three days in winter, the lives of George Caldwell and his son Peter reach crisis-point. A sequence of small disasters (being shot in the foot by a loutish pupil; breaking down in deep snow; having to stay overnight with a colleague he hardly knows) helps George to understand that the point of his existence is his love for his son, and that it is time to surrender the boy to adulthood. For his part, Peter begins to see that his father's exasperating, oblique approach to life is really a defence, that he is not so much a beloved fool as a man pathetically, desperately floundering to stay alive.

UPDIKE, John Hoyer
Born 1932
US citizen
First job: staff reporter, *New Yorker*
Began writing: 1950s
Other details: spent a year as a Rhodes Scholar, studying fine art in Oxford.

OTHER UPDIKE *BOOKS*
Of the Farm
Marry Me
The Poorhouse Fair
Museums and Women (short stories)

Updike began his career writing sleekly witty stories and poems for the *New Yorker*. In one story, he imagines microscopic creatures on a laboratory slide having a cocktail party just like New England commuters. In others, he dissects the farcical, empty sexual shenanigans of real commuters as if they are laboratory animals.

This kind of brilliance spills over into several of Updike's best-known novels. *Couples* describes the pretentious partner-changing of ten couples in a small Connecticut town: musical beds for the chattering classes. In *The Witches of Eastwick* bored housewives set up as amateur witches – and raise a sexy devil. The wracked hero of *A Month of Sundays* is a 'progressive' clergyman who loses faith and discovers sex.

Side by side with work like this, Updike has produced more serious, more tragic books. Their heroes are in a state of psychological panic and anarchy. Nothing is certain for them, except the short-lived pleasure of sex and the inexorable approach of death. Relationships with other people are a source of both comfort and pain. Updike is particularly good at relationships between parents and children – and this is the main theme of *The Centaur*, one of his finest books. Peter Caldwell, a fifteen-year-old high-school student, idolizes his father George. George is a hopeless school-teacher, tormented by pupils and colleagues alike, and the story describes both his self-questioning agony and Peter's gradual realization that his father may have feet of clay –

all refracted through their inarticulate, beautifully-described love for one another.

Updike adds yet another layer. In an existence where getting up to face certain humiliation in the classroom is a daily martyrdom, George sustains himself with the fantasy that he is Chiron, the centaur in Greek myth who taught wisdom to such heroes as Jason and Herakles, who was wounded by a poisoned arrow and finally gave up his immortality to find peace at last in death. This theme never intrudes, but it enriches the story, carries it outside small-town horizons, in a satisfying and wholly Updikeish way.

TRY THESE

Philip Roth, *The Ghost Writer*
Arthur Laurents, *The Way We Were*
Anne Tyler, *Morgan's Passing*
John Irving, *A Prayer for Owen Meany*
Frederic Raphael, *Heaven and Earth*

See also
Grass, Irving, Jolley, Tyler

66 'Knock me down,' the drunk said, smiling so broadly his cheeks gleamed. 'Knock me down when I want to save your soul. Are you ready to die?' This made my father jerk still like a halted movie. The drunk, seeing his triumph, repeated, 'Are you ready to die?'

The drunk nimbly sidestepped to me and put his arms round my waist and gave me a hug ... 'Ah,' he told me, 'you're a good warm body. But you're all skin and bone. Doesn't the old bastard feed you? Hey, you,' he called to my father, 'what sort of an old lech do you call yourself lifting these poor boys off the street with empty stomachs?'

'I thought I was ready to die,' my father said, 'but now I wonder if anybody is. I wonder now if a ninety-nine-year-old Chinaman with tuberculosis, gonorrhea, syphilis, and toothache is ready to die.'

The drunk's fingers began to gouge under my ribs and I jerked out of his grasp. 'Daddy, let's go.'

'No, Peter,' my father said, 'this gentleman is talking sense. Are you ready to die,' he asked the drunk. 'What do you think the answer is?' 99

MARIO VARGAS LLOSA

AUNT JULIA AND THE SCRIPTWRITER (1977)

● ● ● ● ● ● ● ● ● ● ● ● ● ● ●

THE STORY

Mario, an eighteen-year-old law-student and would-be writer, moonlights as news editor for a tinpot radio station in Lima. He is amazed by the personality of Pedro Comacho, the crazed genius who pours out episodes for half a dozen soaps a day, writing, producing and starring in all of them. Every alternate chapter of the novel is a slice from one of Comacho's soaps, and the other chapters concentrate on the 'real' characters. As the book proceeds, Comacho is gradually sucked into his own creations. His reality drains from him like blood – and Mario, watching it happen, is powerless to help because he is engulfed in a real-life soap-opera of his own: a stormy love-affair with his 32-year-old Aunt Julia.

> VARGAS LLOSA, Mario
> Born 1936
> Peruvian citizen
> Began writing: 1960s
> Other details: unsuccessful
> Presidential candidate in
> 1980s.

OTHER VARGAS LLOSA NOVELS

Captain Pantoja and the Special
　Service
The Time of the Hero
The Green House
In Praise of the Stepmother

South Americans are more addicted to soap operas than any other people in the world. In every South American country, local TV and radio stations put out half a dozen, even a dozen, soap operas a day. Their fans are everywhere, from rainforest villages to cardinals' palaces, from shanty-town huts and government offices to military barracks.

Just as the trappings of people's lives in soaps are luxurious – gorgeous clothes, superb houses, lavish banquets – so the events are usually over-the-top. If an average week's episodes fail to bring in incest, madness, blackmail, abortion, murder – not to mention such natural disasters as floods and earthquakes – audience figures drop. South American soaps also specialize in the supernatural: ghosts and spirit visitors are standard characters.

All this is a grown-up version of children's fairy tales, in which ordinary people have adventures which ignore any boundary between the natural world and fantasy. Some fifty years ago, South American novelists developed the idea still further, into a fully-fledged literary style: magic realism. Characters in magic realist books, like those of soaps, include not only the living, but also ghosts of dead relatives, and such giants of the past as Columbus, Bolívar and Beethoven. The characters are faced by terrifying events – political oppression, child abuse, torture, religious mania, murder – and only their imaginations keep them sane. They endure reality by setting the frightful events they live through in the context of a vast mental landscape of even more extraordinary happenings.

Magic realism works by describing fantastic events as if they are real, and real events as if they are fantastic. The result is that every paragraph seems bizarre, every page is hypnotic and the whole experience is rich, strange and intellectually seductive. This is the kind of book Vargas Llosa writes, and in *Aunt Julia and the Scriptwriter* (whose plot actually depends on soap opera) he adds an ingredient rare in South American literature: slapstick. His people scurry about like characters in farce, and what happens to them constantly teeters between the weird, the awful and the plain ridiculous. He lures us with comedy, seduces us with fantasy – and then, unexpectedly, leaves us pondering at the end of the book if tragedy and suffering are any less terrible just because those who experience them are fools.

TRY THESE

Isabel Allende, *The House of the Spirits*

Gabriel García Márquez, *Love in the Time of Cholera*

Angela Carter, *Nights at the Circus*

Salman Rushdie, *Midnight's Children*

Stephen Dobyns, *The Two Deaths of Senora Puccini*

Garrison Keillor, *Radio Romance* (not magic realist, but brilliantly funny about local radio)

OTHER MAGIC REALISTS

Gabriel García Márquez, *One Hundred Years of Solitude*

Alejo Carpentier, *The Chase*

Augusto Roa Bastos, *I the Supreme*

Günter Grass, *The Tin Drum*

See also

Carter, Morris, Winterson

66 I had the impression that I'd poked my nose into the wrong place or was addressing some unknown person, and it took me several seconds to recognise the Bolivian scriptwriter beneath his disguise consisting of a white smock, a surgeon's skullcap, and a long rabbinical black beard. He went on writing impassively, without even looking at me, his back slightly hunched over his desk. After a moment, as though he were pausing between one thought and the next, but without turning his head in my direction, I heard him say in his perfectly placed, tender voice: 'The gynaecologist Alberto de Quinteros is delivering his niece's triplets, and one of the little runts is going to be a breech birth. Can you wait five minutes for me? I'll do a Caesarean on the girl and then I'll go and have a verbena-and-mint tea with you.' 99

KURT VONNEGUT

GALÁPAGOS (1985)

● ● ● ● ● ● ● ● ● ● ● ● ● ● ● ● ●

THE STORY

As the human race lurches through the last few days before the apocalyptic Third World War, a group of ill-assorted people gather in Ecuador for the 'Nature Cruise of the Century' to the Galápagos Islands, where Darwin first formulated his Theory of Evolution. They set sail; the apocalypse happens; their ship becomes a second Noah's Ark, the saving of humankind. They land on Santa Rosalia, with no technology except a computer stuffed with a thousand dead languages and a million quotations, and set about survival. This involves retracing humanity's steps down the evolutionary dead-end which has led to our cunning hands and our big brains – most of whose circuitry, Vonnegut claims, has been devoted to lying, cheating, making money and war and engineering the destruction of the planet: in short, to being 'civilized'.

VONNEGUT, Kurt
Born 1922
US citizen
First jobs: soldier (draftee); reporter
Began writing: late 1940s
Other details: began writing fiction as a hobby while working as PR man for the General Electric Company.

As a twenty-one-year-old prisoner of war, Vonnegut witnessed the firebombing of Dresden during the Second World War, an event which changed his ideas forever. He became, as he puts it, a 'total pessimist', convinced that the human race has evolved beyond redemption, to a point where self-interest and cruelty override all other qualities, and will lead to us destroying both the planet and ourselves with it.

By temperament, however, Vonnegut is not a preacher but a comedian, and he expresses his grim philosophy in surreal, black farce. Because he is sure that our present reality holds out no hope, his books also investigate alternative realities; indeed for a time he wrote (highly unorthodox) science fiction. He even created an alternative fictional personality for himself: the pulp science fiction author Kilgore Trout, who makes an appearance in novel after novel – and in one *(The Sirens of Titan)* is whisked away to the planet of Tralfamadore, a place he has himself invented.

As Vonnegut writes each book, he keeps interrupting himself to make irrelevant remarks, tell jokes, remind us of political events or of important details in this or that character's past or future life. His novels are like shaggy-dog stories, told by someone who feels that the news he has to tell is desperately urgent – but who, when it comes to the point, keeps collapsing into giggles. This rambling surface is, however, deceptive. Vonnegut's stories are crisply, cunningly organized to make his points, and he places each interruption, each joke, for maximum unsettling effect.

Dark humour is a favourite twentieth-century form – as if screaming with laughter at the plight of the world were the only alternative to screaming with despair. In the same way, many artists use surrealism to point up the lethal illogic of the world we actually inhabit. Most dark humour is sharp and savage; most surrealism is dreamlike and bizarre. Writers like Vonnegut – humorists who bumble, rambling surrealists – are rare. Reading his books is like taking a tour inside his head. Nothing seems irrelevant, out-of-date or odd, and yet everything comes as a complete surprise. The most disarming thing of all, perhaps, is that he is such a charming, guileless writer. It is only on reflection that you see that gentleness is, in fact, just one more weapon in a well-stocked, functional and lethal arsenal.

OTHER VONNEGUT NOVELS
Cat's Cradle
Slaughterhouse Five
Breakfast of Champions
Deadeye Dick
Hocus Pocus

TRY THESE
Brian Aldiss, *The Primal Urge*
Frederick Pohl, *The Coming of the Quantum Cats*
Michael Moorcock, *The Final Programme*
Gore Vidal, *Kalki*
Bamber Gascoigne, *Cod Strewth*

See also
Heller, Irving, Science Fiction and Fantasy

❝ MacIntosh was barefoot and wearing nothing but a pair of khaki shorts whose fly was unbuttoned and under which he wore no underwear, so that his penis was no more a secret than the pendulum on a grandfather clock.

Yes, and I pause to marvel now at how little interested this man was in reproduction, in being a huge success biologically – despite his exhibitionistic sexuality and his mania for claiming as his own property as many of the planet's life-supporting systems as possible ... Andrew MacIntosh didn't even care if he himself lived or died – as evidenced by his enthusiasms for skydiving and the racing of high-performance motor vehicles and so on ...

More and more people back then, and not just Andrew MacIntosh, had found ensuring the survival of the human race a total bore.

It was a lot more fun, so to speak, to hit and hit a tennis ball. **❞**

EVELYN WAUGH
A HANDFUL OF DUST (1934)

● ● ● ● ● ● ● ● ● ● ● ● ● ● ● ●

THE STORY
Lady Brenda Last, a hard-as-nails socialite, takes a lover to pass the time. The effect on her husband Tony and son John Andrew is devastating. After a family tragedy, Tony plans to divorce her, but discovers that the alimony will be so high that he will have to sell his beloved family house. He goes on a long trip to Brazil, and is lost in the Amazon jungle, where he finishes up as the prisoner of a mad English settler, reading Dickens aloud.

WAUGH, Evelyn Arthur St John
1902-1966
British citizen
First jobs: prep-school teacher; journalist
Began writing: early teens, first publication (poems) in 1916
Other details: *Diaries, Letters* and novel *The Ordeal of Gilbert Pinfold* give unforgettable picture of a tormented, offensive, dazzlingly witty man almost insane with fury at the way the world is going.

See also
Wodehouse

For 1920s bright young things of the English upper class, it was as if the First World War had been lost, not won. Half a generation had been swept away, and the survivors were haunted by an odd feeling, almost of guilt, at still being alive. Their ethos – the stiff-upper-lip, thrash-the-bounders spirit taught on public-school playing-fields – had proved no match for machine guns and tanks. And worst of all, perhaps, the war had shown that ordinary people – 'other ranks'; the women who worked in the factories – were just as 'important' as their 'betters'.

Thoughts like these led to three different reactions from the upper class. Some shut their eyes to twentieth-century developments altogether, keeping tight grip on their wealth, privilege and invincible self-conceit. Others adapted, making the effort to behave like citizens of an egalitarian democracy. And a third group went on with their chinless-wonder lives, coming-out parties, hunt balls and Fridays-to-Mondays in grand country houses – but now with a previously-unknown sense of desperation, as if there were literally no tomorrow. Waugh was one of the darlings of this third group. He had been to public school and Oxford. He was a clubman, a race-goer, a welcome dinner-guest. But he was also an outsider: not upper-class, not wealthy, and above all a writer, sending up the very Hooray Henrys and Henriettas with whom he spent his time.

Perhaps because he was one himself, Waugh the novelist was particularly interested in the misfits in high society: people who worked for their living (usually in jobs light-years away from the social pretensions of their leisure activities), or members of 'great' families who felt out of tune with the traditions of their class. His characters are fools; the incidents he invents are ludicrous; his books are farce. But the underlying tone is tragic: when Waugh's characters are hurt – unlike, say P.G. Wodehouse's – they bleed. In 1930 he was converted to Roman Catholicism, and stirred ideas of original sin, of the inborn guilt of the entire human race, into an already sombre mix.

OTHER WAUGH NOVELS
Decline and Fall
Scoop
Brideshead Revisited
'Sword of Honour' trilogy (more serious: about upper-class officers in the Second World War)

TRY THESE
Anthony Powell, *From a View to a Death*
Aldous Huxley, *Crome Yellow*
F. Scott Fitzgerald, *The Great Gatsby* (similar society, similar period, similar dazzle and wit, but set in US and distinctly grimmer)
Paul Micou, *The Music Programme*

> That evening as usual she telephoned to Hetton. 'I'm talking from the flat.'
>
> 'Oh, ah.' ...
>
> 'Tony, you must be nice about it. It's all so exciting – front door and a latch-key and all ... And someone sent me a lot of flowers today – so many that there's hardly room for them and I've had to put them in the basin on account of having no pots. It wasn't you, was it?'
>
> 'Yes ... as a matter of fact.'
>
> 'Darling, I did so hope it was ... how like you.' ...
>
> 'When are you coming back?'
>
> 'Almost at once. Good night, my sweet.'
>
> 'What a lot of talk,' said Beaver. All the time she was speaking, she had been kept busy with one hand warding him off the telephone, which he threatened playfully to disconnect.
>
> 'Wasn't it sweet of Tony to send all those flowers?'
>
> 'I'm not awfully fond of Tony.'
>
> 'Don't let that worry you, my beauty, he doesn't like you at all.'

Jeanette Winterson

Sexing the Cherry (1989)

● ● ● ● ● ● ● ● ● ● ● ● ● ● ● ●

THE STORY

Alternate chapters concern the Dog Woman and her son Jordan. The Dog Woman is a giantess in 17th-century London, fiercely loyal to Charles I, who develops a passion for tearing men apart – any men, but particularly her 'lovers' and the Puritans who executed Charles. Jordan is a naturalist who sails with the plant-collector John Tradescant and has dream-adventures in countries populated by princesses who live beyond the reach of gravity. Just when you think you have the measure of the book, Winterson swings us into the 20th century – and shows us, conjurer-like, that reality is illusion, dreams are waking, and fiction is no more than another kind of truth.

○ **WINTERSON, Jeanette**
○ **Born 1959**
○ **British citizen**
○ **Began writing: 1980s**
○ **Other details: brought up as**
○ **a Pentecostal Evangelist;**
○ **before she went to Oxford**
○ **worked selling ice-cream,**
○ **making up corpses in a**
○ **mortuary and washing floors**
○ **in a mental hospital.**

TRY THESE

Michèle Roberts, *The Book of Mrs Noah* (another slant on Noah's Ark)

Hilary Mantel, *Fludd*

Bamber Gascoigne, *Cod Strewth*

Bernice Rubens, *Our Father*

See also

Adams, Carter, Morris, Vargas Llosa

Winterson's first novel, *Oranges Are Not the Only Fruit*, was the bleak story of a girl brought up by joyless Christian fundamentalists who finds happiness in a lesbian love-affair. Dozens of other authors have written about the quest for happiness in an oppressive world. But Winterson's detail makes her book unique. She is particularly good about about the way fundamentalists can seem, to non-believers, like visitors from Mars – and how this feeling wracks the heroine, torn between love for her appalling, ludicrous mother and scorn for what she does. Two other Winterson touches are the way she treats lesbianism not defiantly (as it normally is in novels), but entirely matter-of-fact and normal – and the way the heroine blows this feeling apart by abandoning her love-affair at the end of the story, shedding it as determinedly as she already shed her family.

Similar themes – search for happiness; the ordinariness of the unusual; the oppressiveness of convention – are present in every Winterson novel, though their treatment each time is wildly different. *The Passion* balances the story of a young French peasant whose life is fulfilled – or not – when he becomes personal chef to Napoleon, with the account of a lesbian love-affair, one of whose partners is the web-footed daughter of a Venetian fisherman. The setting of *Boating for Beginners* is Old Testament Nineveh – uprooted and dumped in a modern world of supermarkets, women's magazines, afternoon TV and chipolata sausages. In this novel, God is not only the Supreme Deity but a publicity-seeking author; the Flood is a publicity stunt dreamed up to promote his latest book, *Genesis*, and Noah is a crackpot inventor, whose Ark is just one of many wheezes.

Some critics have claimed that it is outrageous to fiddle in this way with readers' normal expectations of what 'stories' and 'reality' are – and if that is so, *Sexing the Cherry* is the most outrageous, most astonishing book even Winterson has ever written. It is about all kinds of things: the 'pull' human beings feel between the need for dreams and the need for action; the awfulness of evangelical religion; the plight of women (and the predicament of men); the lies people tell under the guise of history. Serious themes, perhaps, but the telling combines folk-tale-like fantasy with sardonic, ruthless humour. If one of the grimmer Grimm's fairy stories had collided, and had been inextricably intertwined, with *Catch-22*, *Sexing the Cherry* might well have been what came of it.

● ● ● ● ● ● ● ● ● ● ● ● ● ● ● ● ● ● ● ●

> " I was his falcon. I hung on his arm and fed at his hand. He said my nose was sharp and cruel and that my eyes had madness in them. He said I would tear him into pieces if he dealt softly with me ...
>
> His game was to have me sit astride him when we made love and hold me tight in the small of my back. He said he had to have me above him, in case I picked his eyes out in the faltering candlelight.
>
> I was none of these things but I became them.
>
> At night, in June I think, I flew off his wrist and tore his liver from his body, and bit my chain in pieces and left him on the bed with his eyes open.
>
> He looked surprised, I don't know why. As your lover describes you, so you are. "

P. G. WODEHOUSE

JOY IN THE MORNING (1963)

● ● ● ● ● ● ● ● ● ● ● ● ● ● ● ●

THE STORY

Bertie's chum Boko Fittleworth
wants to marry Nobby Hopwood.
Unfortunately, Nobby's guardian
Lord Worpledon can't stand the
sight of Boko. To help things along,
Bertie and Jeeves go down to
Steeple Bumpleigh (where all the
other parties live) – despite the fact
that the village crawls with people
like Florence Cray (the Amazon who
thinks Bertie should be engaged to
her), Stilton Cheeswright (who
thinks that Florence should be
engaged to him) and Edwin the Boy
Scout (who thinks that other people
exist solely to be the victims of his
Good Deeds). The outcome is
chaos (not least a fancy-dress ball
in which a Sinbad-the-Sailor
costume, complete with ginger
whiskers, plays a vital role).
Fortunately, Jeeves is on hand, his
brain well-fuelled with fish ...

● WODEHOUSE, Pelham Grenville
● 1881-1975
● British/US citizen
● First job: bank clerk
● Began writing: 1890s
● Other details: wrote dialogue
● and lyrics for some of
● 1920s-30s Broadway
● musicals; nickname was
● 'Plum'.

See also
Jerome, Waugh

Every Wodehouse novel – and there are
over 90 – uses the same sublimely simple
basic plot. Two young people, who want to
get married, are hindered by some obstacle
(lack of money, for example, or the disap-
proval of relatives), but eventually succeed.

This rock-solid foundation, each time,
supports a tower of farcical confusion.
Wodehouse invented complications like a
manic conjuror. In order to win the girl, his
hero has to track down terrifying guardians
(harumphing uncles, dragon-like aunts) in
their lairs (usually large country houses full
of eccentric guests). He may have to pre-
tend to be someone else (a visiting US mil-
lionaire; an Amazon explorer; a detective; a
Harley Street psychiatrist). He could be
called on to steal a necklace, purloin a letter
or kidnap a pig. If all else fails, he may
need to set up some kind of brave rescue:
pulling some spluttering grandee out of the
pond into which he (the hero) has just sur-
reptitiously pushed him.

In fantasy-quests, the heroes are usually
handicapped by puniness. In Wodehouse
novels, their problem is lack of brains.
They are upper-class twits, superb with tennis rackets and golf clubs, knowledgeable
about what they call browsin' and sluicin',
but unable even to tie their own shoelaces
or deliver a letter without assistance. They
are no match for the suspicious secretaries,
curmudgeonly constables, overbearing but-
lers and hawk-eyed housemaids (most of
them detectives in disguise) who infest each
Wodehouse castle and its grounds.

Fortunately, in every book, help is at

hand: someone of superior brain-power who comes to the rescue when all seems lost. In Wodehouse's Bertie Wooster novels, that rescuer is Jeeves. Jeeves is Bertie's manservant – wise, devious and unflappable (unless Bertie grows a moustache, wears rainbow spats or practises the trombone). Never mind that every one of Jeeves' schemes dumps the young master even deeper in the soup; never mind that Bertie always ends up bruised, soaked and insulted. In Wodehouse's fantasy-land, as in Tom and Jerry cartoons, no one is ever really hurt, and the characters jump up smiling after every disaster, to stride cheerfully forward to face the next catastrophe.

OTHER JEEVES BOOKS
The Inimitable Jeeves
What Ho, Jeeves
Jeeves in the Offing
The Code of the Woosters
The Little Nugget

THE BLANDINGS SAGA
Wodehouse's other main series is set in Blandings Castle, home of Lord Emsworth, his prize pig The Empress, his Gorgon-like sisters, and a menagerie of guests (poets, newt-fanciers, silent-film magnates, prep-school headmasters), all of whom are there for more than just a holiday. The books include *Leave it to Psmith*, *Summer Lightning*, *Galahad at Blandings*, *Heavy Weather*, *Pigs Have Wings* and *Uncle Fred in the Springtime*.

66 'Did you know that I was once engaged to Florence?'
'Of course.'
'And now Stilton is.'
'Yes.'
'How absolutely extraordinary. It's like one of those great race movements you read about.'
'I suppose it's her profile that does it. She has a lovely profile.'
'Seen from the left.'
'Seen from the right, too.'
'Well, yes, in a measure, seen from the right, too. But would that account for it? I mean, in these busy days you can't spend your whole time dodging round a girl, trying to see her sideways. I still maintain that this tendency on the part of the populace to get engaged to Florence is inexplicable. And that made Uncle Percy a bit frosty to Boko?'
'Glacial.' 99

ACKNOWLEDGEMENTS

● ●

Page 3, from *The Hitch Hiker's Guide to the Galaxy* © Douglas Adams 1979, reproduced by permission of Pan Books Ltd; page 5, from *The Handmaid's Tale* © Margaret Atwood 1985, reproduced by permission of Random House (UK) Ltd. Permission to reprint in the United States granted by Houghton Mifflin Company, and in Canada by McClelland and Stewart; page 11, from *Oscar and Lucinda* © Peter Carey 1988, reproduced by permission of Faber and Faber Ltd and University of Queensland Press; page 13, from *Nights at the Circus* © Angela Carter 1984, reproduced by permission of the estate of the author and Chatto and Windus; page 15, from *Prizzi's Glory* © Richard Condon 1988, reproduced by permission of Michael Joseph Ltd, Abner Stein and Dutton, an imprint of New American Library, a division of Penguin Books USA Inc; page 15, from *A Taste For Death* © P. D. James 1986, reproduced with kind permission of Elaine Greene Ltd: first published in Great Britain by Faber and Faber Ltd, in the United States by Alfred A. Knopf Inc, in Canada by Lester & Orpen Dennys Ltd; page 17, from *The Dead of Jericho* © Colin Dexter 1981, reproduced by permission of Macmillan London; page 23, from *Rebecca*, reproduced by permission of Doubleday, a division of Bantam, Doubleday, Dell Publishing Group Inc, and by permission of Curtis Brown on behalf of the estate of Daphne Du Maurier, © Daphne Du Maurier, 1938; page 25, from *Niccolò Rising* © Dorothy Dunnett 1986, reproduced by permission of Michael Joseph Ltd and Alfred A. Knopf Inc, a division of Random House Inc; page 27, from *My Family and Other Animals* by Gerald M. Durrell © 1957, renewed © 1985 by Gerald M. Durrell. Used by permission of Viking Penguin, a division of Penguin Books USA Inc, and Rupert Hart-Davis, an imprint of HarperCollins Publishers Ltd; page 29, from *Pawn of Prophecy* © David Eddings 1931, reproduced by permission of Transworld Publishers Ltd and Ballantine Books Inc, a division of Random House Inc; page 33, from *Lady's Maid* © Margaret Forster 1990, reproduced by permission of Chatto and Windus and Doubleday, a division of Bantam, Doubleday, Dell Publishing Group Inc; page 35, from *The French Lieutenant's Woman* © John Fowles 1969, first published by Jonathan Cape Ltd; published in paperback by Picador; page 37, from *My Brilliant Career* © Miles Franklin 1901, reproduced by permission of Virago Press; page 39, from *The Queen of the Tambourine* © Jane Gardam 1991, published by Sinclair-Stevenson Ltd; page 41, from *Coromandel Sea Change* © Rumer Godden 1991, reproduced by permission of Macmillan London; page 43, from *Lord of the Flies* © William Golding 1954, reproduced by permission of Faber and Faber Ltd and Harcourt Brace Jovanovich Inc; page 45, from *Cat and Mouse* © Günter Grass 1961, reproduced by permission of Martin Secker and Warburg Ltd and Luchterhand Literaturverlag GmbH, Hamburg; page 47, from *I, Claudius* © Robert Graves 1934, reproduced by permission of A.P. Watt Ltd on behalf of the Trustees of the Robert Graves Copyright Trust; page 49, from *Brighton Rock* © 1938 Verdant SA, reproduced by permission of William Heinemann Ltd; page 53, from *Catch-22* © Joseph Heller 1961, reproduced by permission of Rogers, Coleridge and White Ltd; page 55, from *Cotillion* © 1953 by Georgette Heyer, © renewed 1981 by Richard George Rougier, reproduced by permission of Heron Enterprises Ltd; page 57, from *Ripley's Game* © Patricia Highsmith 1974, reproduced by permission of William Heinemann; page 61, from *The World According to Garp* © John Irving 1978, reproduced by permission of Victor Gollancz Ltd and Dutton, an imprint of New American Library, a division of Penguin Books USA Inc; page 63, from *The Summer Book* © Tove Jansson 1972; page 67, from *Miss Peabody's Inheritance* © Elizabeth Jolley 1983, reproduced by permission of Penguin Books Ltd; page 69, from *A Perfect Spy* © John le Carré 1986, reproduced by permission of Hodder and Stoughton; page 71, from *Freaky Deaky* © Elmore Leonard 1988, reproduced by permission of Penguin Books Ltd; page 73, from *Doves and Silk Handkerchiefs* © G. H. Morris 1986, reproduced by permission of Constable and Company Ltd; page 75, from *A House for Mr Biswas* © V.S. Naipaul 1961; page 77, from *The Painter of Signs* © R. K. Narayan 1976, first published in Great Britain by William Heinemann Ltd; page 79, from *Bitter Medicine* © Sara Paretsky 1987, reproduced by permission of Victor Gollancz Ltd and William Morrow & Co Inc; page 81, from *The Colour of Magic* © Terry Pratchett 1983, reproduced by permission of Colin Smythe Ltd, Publishers; page 83, from *The King Must Die* © Mary Renault 1958, reproduced by permission of Longman Group UK; page 85, from *Tilly Trotter* © Catherine Cookson 1980, published by William Heinemann Ltd; page 87, from *Rendezvous With Rama* © Arthur C. Clarke 1973, reprinted by permission of the author and the author's agents, Scott Meredith Literary Agency Inc, 845 Third Avenue, New York 10022, and by permission of Victor Gollancz Ltd; page 91, from *The Patience of Maigret* © Georges Simenon 1965, reproduced by permission of Administration de l'ouevre de Georges Simenon; page 95, from *The Agony and the Ecstasy* © Irving Stone 1961, reproduced by permission of Doubleday, a division of Bantam, Doubleday, Dell Publishing Inc; page 97, from *The Lord of the Rings* © George Allen and Unwin (Publishers) 1954, now HarperCollins Publishers Ltd. Permission to reprint in the United States granted by Houghton Mifflin Company; page 103, from *Morgan's Passing* © Anne Tyler 1980, reproduced by permission of Chatto and Windus and Random House Inc; page 105 from *The Centaur* © John Updike 1963, reproduced by permission of Penguin Books Ltd; page 107, from *Aunt Julia and the Scriptwriter* © Mario Vargas Llosa 1977, reproduced by permission of Faber and Faber Ltd and Agencia literaria Carmen Balcells, Barcelona; page 109, from *Galápagos* © Kurt Vonnegut 1985, reproduced by permission of Dell, a division of Bantam, Doubleday, Dell Publishing; page 111, from *A Handful of Dust* © Evelyn Waugh 1934, reproduced by permission of Peters, Fraser and Dunlop; page 113, from *Sexing the Cherry* © Jeanette Winterson 1985, reproduced by permission of Bloomsbury Publishing and Alfred A. Knopf Inc, a division of Random House Inc; page 115, from *Joy in the Morning* © P. G. Wodehouse 1963, reproduced by permission of A. P. Watt Ltd on behalf of the Trustees of the Wodehouse Estate, and by permission of Hutchinson Books Ltd.